A Traveller's Guide to
NORMAN BRITAIN

A Traveller's Guide to
NORMAN BRITAIN

Trevor Rowley & Michael Cyprien

HTI

Historical Times INC.
Harrisburg

CONTENTS

First published in 1986 by Historical Times Incorporated,
2245 Kohn Road, Harrisburg, PA 17105, USA
and by Routledge & Kegan Paul plc
14 Leicester Square, London WC2H 7PH, England
9 Park Street, Boston, Mass. 02108, USA
464 St Kilda Road, Melbourne, Victoria 3004, Australia, and
Broadway House, Newton Road, Henley on Thames, Oxon RG9 1EN, England

Text by Trevor Rowley
Consultant Editor Dr Charles Kightly
Photography and Art Direction by Michael Cyprien

Filmset in England by BAS Printers Limited,
Over Wallop, Stockbridge, Hampshire
Printed in England by Balding + Mansell Limited
Wisbech, Cambridgeshire

Library of Congress Cataloguing in Publication Data

Rowley, Trevor, 1942–
    A traveller's guide to Norman Britain.
    Includes index.
    1. Normans—Great Britain—Antiquities—Guide books.
2. Great Britain—Description and travel—
1971–   —Guide-books.   3. Great Britain—History,
Local. I. Cyprien, Michael. II. Title. III. Title:
Norman Britain.
DA195.R87   1986   914.1′04858   85-27336
ISBN 0-918678-11-0

INTRODUCTION

Well over nine centuries after the event, the Norman Conquest remains a subject of pressing interest and fiercely-argued controversy among all those interested in British history. To some, the mention of 1066 conjures up a vision of clean-living and liberty-loving Anglo-Saxon heroes, unfairly defeated and brutally enslaved by grasping Norman land-grabbers, who then proceeded to establish a state where might was right and the sword was the law: a vision, incidentally, which they share with the Levellers of Cromwell's day, who attributed all the ills of England to the "Norman Yoke" imposed by the Conqueror and his henchmen. Others, conversely, see pre-Conquest England as a crumbling and moribund nation over-ripe for reform – a backwater populated by ale-swilling rustics, ignorant priests and turbulent half-Viking warlords, sorely in need of the forward-looking Normans to bring it into line with the rest of civilised Europe. Even among sober academics, opinion is sharply divided between those who hold that the Normans were basically efficent barbarians, whose success in ruling England depended heavily on their use of already-existing Anglo-Saxon institutions: and those who hail them as brilliant innovators, upon whose work all that was best in medieval England rested.

What cannot be questioned, however, is that the Norman Conquest utterly transformed English society – as its repercussions were later, and to a lesser extent, to affect those of Wales and lowland Scotland. The most sweeping change, and that which struck contemporaries most forcibly, was the extinction or dispossession of the old Anglo-Saxon aristocracy, so that by the end of the Conqueror's reign only two principal landowners were of English origin: and at the same time landed wealth was concentrated in the hands of a small but immensely powerful group of men, so that in 1086 some 40% of England was controlled by a mere thirty-two Norman magnates, many of them kinsmen or close friends of King William. Scarcely less dramatic, though it came about rather more slowly, was the Norman takeover of the English church: which is best demonstrated by the fact that, at the time of the Conqueror's death, only one English bishopric and two English abbeys were ruled by Englishmen. All other senior ecclesiastical posts had passed to clerics who were Norman either by birth or education, and who were determined to impose Norman reforms on what they regarded as a hopelessly old-fashioned and corrupt institution – though few were quite as militant as Abbot Thurstan of Glastonbury, whose disputes with his monks about the proper style of chanting culminated in a pitched battle within the abbey church itself.

To what extent Norman influence filtered down to the lower reaches of society is less clear, though it is worth remembering that the invaders were never more than a tiny minority – it has been estimated that some 10,000 Normans settled in England during the Conqueror's reign, the total population being perhaps $1\frac{1}{2}$ million – and that by their nature they constituted a ruling rather than a subservient class. It is notable, moreover, that while Norman-French almost totally ousted English from the palace, the manor-house and the law court (in whose vocabulary, as Professor Loyn has noted, "gallows" and "outlaw" were virtually the only English words to survive); and while it heavily influenced the terminology of commerce and town life, the tongue of the conquerors apparently had remarkably little effect on the language of village and farm. There – to quote a familiar but still telling example – the peasants continued to tend their English "sheep", "swine" and "cattle", and only when these came to be served up at the manor house table were they transformed into the Norman-French "mutton", "pork" and "beef".

For the modern traveller, however, the architectural rather than the cultural or political legacy of the Normans will be of greatest interest: and indeed he need rarely seek very far for reminders of how firmly and enduringly they set their physical mark on the face of Britain. If, for example, there is a pre-Victorian church in the town or village where he finds himself, it will more than probably retain some distinctively Norman feature – be it a fragment of sculpture, a font, or a complete pillared nave – and in not a few cases the entire structure will be substantially Norman. If there is a medieval cathedral or monastery nearby, the first is likely to have been rebuilt and the second founded during the Norman period: and if, most tellingly of all, there is a castle in the vicinity, in nine cases out of ten this too will have been begun by the Normans. For, as this book demonstrates again and again, it was through their architecture that the Normans most lastingly expressed their determination to dominate their conquered realm: and the great pillars of a Norman cathedral or the elaborately carved doorway of a Norman parish church symbolised, in their own way, the triumph of the new order as effectively as the frowning walls of the Tower of London or Colchester Castle.

Through Norman architecture, too, and under the author's expert guidance, the traveller can not only trace the progress of the Conquest from its beginnings at Pevensey in 1066 to the compilation of Domesday Book twenty years later: but also see how the Anglo-

Norman state developed during the twelfth century, producing in the process increasingly accomplished and beautiful churches and stronger and more formidable fortresses. The author's careful selection of castles, for instance, demonstrates how the Normans used their talent for fortification first to secure southeast England and protect their vital communications with their homeland: and later to hold down their newly-won kingdom, while defending its frontiers against the threat of invasion from Scandinavia and Scotland. Well respresented, likewise, are the castles, abbeys and planned towns which enabled the Norman Marcher lords to extend their power into the heart of Wales: and the splendid architectural monuments of the Norman clerics and knights who peacefully infiltrated southern Scotland under the patronage of the Scottish kings.

Armed with this guidebook, the traveller will also find it easy to follow in the footsteps of those spiritual warriors of Norman Britain, the monks who colonised the wastelands of Yorkshire and Cumbria, braved the gales and sea-raiders of Lindisfarne, or served one of the great cathedrals rebuilt by reforming Norman bishops: and with it he may seek out the smaller but no less fascinating Norman churches which may be hidden in such out-of-the-way places as Barfreston in Kent or Culbone in Somerset. But whether he chooses to journey to remote shrines like Pennant Melangell among the Welsh hills, or rather to explore famous showplaces like the White Tower of London, Dover Castle, or the crypt of Canterbury Cathedral, the traveller will always be aware that he is in the presence of a great and unique race of men – the Normans.

The author of this book, Trevor Rowley, M.A, M.Litt., FSA, MIFA, is an acknowledged expert on Norman England. A geography graduate of University College, London, he is at present Staff Tutor in Archeology and Local Studies at the Oxford University Department for External Studies. Among his many other publications are *Villages in the Landscape* (Dent 1978); *The Norman Heritage* (Routledge 1983); and *The High Middle Ages* (Routledge 1985).

During his extensive career in publishing, Michael Cyprien has produced many popular books on a wide variety of subjects. Not only has he devised and designed this series of historical Traveller's Guides but, in collaboration with their individual authors, motors many thousands of miles, and walks over hundreds of sites to take the photographs with which each title is so fully illustrated.

The excellent Ordnance Survey Landranger maps will prove invaluable in locating the sites described. These maps are widely available: and their reference numbers and National Grid coordinates accompany each site entry.

Charles Kightly, York 1986

1 Adel Church
2 Appleby
3 Arbroath Abbey
4 Bamburgh Castle
5 Barfreston Church
6 Barnard Castle
7 Battle Abbey
8 Berkhamsted
9 Blyth Priory
10 Boothby Pagnell
11 Brougham Castle
12 Buildwas Abbey
13 Burton Agnes
14 Bury St Edmunds
15 Cambridge
16 Carisbrooke Castle
17 Carlisle
18 Cartmel Priory
19 Castle Acre
20 Castle Rising
21 Charney Basset
22 Chepstow Castle
23 Chester Cathedral
24 Christchurch
25 Clun
26 Colchester Castle
27 Corfe Castle
28 Culbone
29 Dalmeny
30 Dover Castle
31 Dryburgh Abbey
32 Dunfermline Abbey
33 Durham
34 East Meon
35 Edinburgh Castle
36 Ely Cathedral
37 Ewenny
38 Fountains Abbey
39 Furness Abbey
40 Gloucester Cathedral
41 Goodrich Castle
42 Hardham Church
43 Heath Chapel
44 Hereford Cathedral
45 Iffley Church
46 Isleham Priory
47 Jedburgh Abbey
48 Kenilworth Castle
49 Kidwelly
50 Kirkham Priory
51 Kirkstall Abbey
52 Lewes
53 Lincoln
54 Lindisfarne Priory
55 Llanstephan Castle
56 Tower of London
57 Ludlow
58 Lydford
59 Malmesbury
60 Melbourne Church
61 Melrose Abbey
62 Much Wenlock Priory
63 Norham

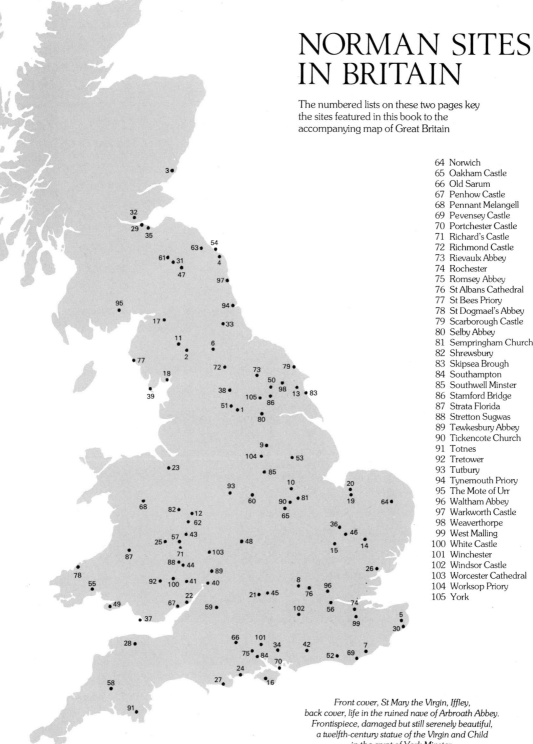

NORMAN SITES IN BRITAIN

The numbered lists on these two pages key the sites featured in this book to the accompanying map of Great Britain

64 Norwich
65 Oakham Castle
66 Old Sarum
67 Penhow Castle
68 Pennant Melangell
69 Pevensey Castle
70 Portchester Castle
71 Richard's Castle
72 Richmond Castle
73 Rievaulx Abbey
74 Rochester
75 Romsey Abbey
76 St Albans Cathedral
77 St Bees Priory
78 St Dogmael's Abbey
79 Scarborough Castle
80 Selby Abbey
81 Sempringham Church
82 Shrewsbury
83 Skipsea Brough
84 Southampton
85 Southwell Minster
86 Stamford Bridge
87 Strata Florida
88 Stretton Sugwas
89 Tewkesbury Abbey
90 Tickencote Church
91 Totnes
92 Tretower
93 Tutbury
94 Tynemouth Priory
95 The Mote of Urr
96 Waltham Abbey
97 Warkworth Castle
98 Weaverthorpe
99 West Malling
100 White Castle
101 Winchester
102 Windsor Castle
103 Worcester Cathedral
104 Worksop Priory
105 York

Front cover, St Mary the Virgin, Iffley,
back cover, life in the ruined nave of Arbroath Abbey.
Frontispiece, damaged but still serenely beautiful,
a twelfth-century statue of the Virgin and Child
in the crypt of York Minster.

ADEL CHURCH

Leeds, West Yorkshire
OS 104 SE 275402

The village of Adel is on the northern fringe of the Leeds conurbation, four and a half miles north-north-west of Leeds city centre. It is reached either via signposted roads turning east off the A660 Leeds-Bramhope road, or turning north off the A6120 Leeds bypass in the Weetwood area. The church is to the north of the village.

The church of St John the Baptist at Adel (now virtually a suburb of Leeds) was built in *c.*1150, and is one of the finest examples of a Norman parish church to be found anywhere in the country. The south door, with its elaborate decorative motifs of leaves, animals and chevrons, is of particular interest because of the panel showing Christ in Majesty flanked by the symbols of the Evangelists which surmounts it. The chancel arch, again with figured sculptural decora-

tion, incorporates an unusual 'Evil figure' which on the north side is drinking holy water, but on the south is shown cowering away in the face of Christ's victory over death. Most remarkable of all is the original Norman bronze door ring, depicting a monster head holding a tiny bearded man in its mouth. The church of Adel thus contains interesting symbolism, and though some of its meaning is obvious to us, much may have been far clearer to Anglo-Norman observers.

Elaborately carved with characteristic zig-zag and animal-head motifs, the south doorway of Adel church typifies the Norman love of sumptuous entrance portals. The stone was mortared into position before the sculptors set to work. Above right, a monster swallows a man on this Norman door ring at Adel. Far right, fantastic beasts and knights jostle one another on the chancel arch.

The pleasant Cumbrian market town of Appleby falls quite clearly into two portions, separated by the River Eden. On the eastern bank is the original Saxon settlement, with its now redundant church of St Michael in Bongate: the existing fabric of this building dates from the twelfth century and later, but a Saxon hogback tombstone set above its north-west door (now a window) most probably indicates that a church and graveyard stood here before the Norman Conquest. Some fifty years after that event, in about 1110, the Norman lord Ranulf de Meschines founded a new town called Boroughgate on the opposite side of the river, and this is today represented by the wide street of that name, which runs between the castle gates and the church of St. Lawrence. This church, at the north or downhill end of Boroughgate, has been much altered, but still retains the lower part of its original massively-built Norman

tower, most probably designed as a place of refuge. The whole of Boroughgate, indeed, is even now accessible only at a few easily-defended points, so that the entire new Norman town could quickly be turned into a fortress.

At the top of Boroughgate hill stands Appleby Castle, impressively sited on a steep bank above the river and protected on the townward side by a system of baileys and water-filled moats. The original castle was probably founded at the same time as the new town, but its oldest surviving building is the delightful toy-fort-like tower keep built in the later twelfth century, surrounded by a curtain wall of similar date. Other parts of the castle, reconstructed in later Stuart times, contain fine architecture of that period: but it is the Norman tower keep which remains most memorable.

APPLEBY Cumbria
OS 91 NY 685200

Appleby is just off the main A66 road across the Pennines, and is fourteen miles south-east of Penrith and junction 40 of the M6 motorway. It is also famous for its Horse Fair, the greatest gypsy gathering in Britain, held annually during the second week in June.

9

ARBROATH ABBEY Tayside
OS 54 NO 644410

Arbroath Abbey is in the centre of the town, which stands on the east coast of Scotland and the A92, seventeen miles north-east of Dundee.

Arbroath was founded by William the Lion in 1178 as a Tironensian house dedicated to St. Thomas Becket. The Tironensian monks, from the early twelfth century abbey of Kelso, represented a reform movement of the Benedictine and Cluniac traditions led by Bernard of Poitiers. Dissatisfied with the abbey of Cluny, Bernard retired to the forest of Tiron, near Chartres, where in a monastic rule stressing simplicity and manual work he rapidly gained followers. The new order encouraged crafts rather than agricultural labour and thus attracted skilled artisans. From the twelfth century the order grew rapidly in Scotland, with four large abbeys and two priories. Architecturally their buildings achieve a notable unity of style which combines simplicity with a bold handling of scale, and at Arbroath these characteristics are well demonstrated in the west front and the south transept.

Approaching the abbey from the town, the deeply recessed round arch of the west door contrasts with the pointed arches of two later thirteenth century abbey gatehouses, emphasising the Romanesque qualities of the former. Two great towers flank the west front whilst opening behind onto the nave, as arches of the main arcading. Above the plain ornament of the arch, a barrel vault carries a Galilee porch opening through six narrow pointed arches to the nave and three projecting gables to the west. Between the interior arcade and the present exterior arches, simple columns support the passage. Above the whole there was a great circular window, but only the lower part of this survives.

The south transept survives to its full height and is dominated by its soaring lancet windows and an immense round window in the wall top. Positioned in the gable, the round window would have lit only the roof space and its function was therefore primarily aesthetic. The exterior echoes the great west facade. The internal wall surfaces have been used most imaginatively for sculptural effect.

For the most part the cloister ranges do not survive, but there remains a fine example of a late twelfth century vaulted undercroft or cellar below the site museum. This building is known as the Abbot's House.

The multiple pointed arches of "blank arcading" at Abroath Abbey echo the pointed lancet windows above.

BAMBURGH CASTLE
Northumberland
OS 75 NU 184350

Bamburgh Castle stands on the north-east coast of Northumberland, twenty-four miles south-east of the Scottish border and Berwick-on-Tweed. It is reached from the main A1 trunk road via either the B1341 or the B1342 from Belford. Nearby are the Farne Islands and Holy Island. Bamburgh's medieval church, with its monument to the heroine Grace Darling, is also worth a visit.

Possibly the most famous castle on the north-east coast of England, Bamburgh stands high up on a 150 foot cliff, between the village and the sea: it overlooks both and is visible for many miles around. The castle occupies a long and narrow site and consists of a twelfth century keep and three baileys, with some very impressive curtain walling.

Although the present castle was largely built in the Norman period, Bamburgh had long been a defensive site, and also a royal residence from the early seventh century. According to Bede, King Ethelfrith of Northumbria gave the fortress to his wife Bebba, and its present name may be a derivative of *Bebbanburgh*. The fortress was sacked by both Vikings and Scots in the tenth and eleventh centuries.

When William the Conqueror created the fief of Northumberland, he kept Bamburgh as a royal residence. The rock was fortified again in the late eleventh century, probably with a wooden tower, although there is some early stonework in the present castle which could belong to this period. Henry II strengthened the defences and built the massive stone keep, which has the unusual feature of the principal entrance being located on the ground floor. The remains of a twelfth century chapel may be seen in the eastern bailey.

In June 1464 Bamburgh became the first English castle to surrender to cannon, and by 1704 (when it was purchased by Lord Crewe) it was a ruin. It was heavily over-restored in late Victorian times, and today it is the residence of Lord Armstrong.

Bamburgh's mighty Norman keep towers above the sand dunes of the Northumberland coast.

Biting its own tail, a beast guards the simple north doorway of Barfreston church, now blocked.

BARFRESTON CHURCH
Kent
OS 179 TR 264501
Barfreston church is situated amid splendid Kentish countryside, in a scattered hamlet six miles north-north-east of Dover and ten miles south-east of Canterbury. It is well signposted, and can be reached via minor roads turning eastwards off the main A2 Dover-Canterbury road, or westwards (via Eythorne) off the A256 road from Dover to Sandwich.

11

St. Nicholas is the best-preserved Norman church in Kent. It is a small simple building consisting of a nave and chancel, and dates from about 1180. It was built primarily of Caen stone imported from Normandy, and has elaborate carved decorations, similar to those at Kilpeck in Herefordshire and Tickencote in Leicestershire. These are to be found both inside and outside the church. The south doorway has striking carvings of the signs of the Zodiac and the Labours of the Months, while the big 'wheel' window at the east end is also a noticeable feature. At the east end there is also a carved figure of a mounted knight, a well known French motif of the same period. This, and other twelfth century churches in Kent with similar decorations, indicates the existence of a school of Norman sculptors working in the area at that time, influenced no doubt by the masons of the cathedrals at Canterbury and Rochester, where the carvings have parallels.

Carvings of the signs of the Zodiac and the Labours of the Months surround the figure of Christ in Majesty above Barfreston's south door. Right, the splendid east end of the church, with its "wheel" window flanked to the left by a mounted knight. The blank arches below the row of heads are purely decorative but those at ground level serve as buttresses.

The castle is named after its founder Bernard de Balliol, and its earthworks probably date from the 1090s, after William the Conqueror had created an estate here for the house of Balliol. A stone castle was built in c.1125–40 and much of the surviving masonry dates from that period, although it was refortified in the early fourteenth century when the Great Hall was also added. The Bishop of Durham regarded the Balliols as a threat and seized the castle after the fall of John Balliol, king of Scotland, in 1296. Five years later Edward I seized it from the bishop, granting it to the Earls of Warwick through whom it ultimately passed to Richard III. Alterations were made to the castle throughout this period, but it was hardly used after the fourteenth century, and in the sixteenth century the Vane family dismantled many of the buildings for stone to repair Raby Castle.

This is a fine example of an important strategic stronghold, standing high on the craggy bank of the River Tees, and controlling the river crossing: as the present curtain walling, the great round tower, the setting, and the size of the precinct suggest, the castle was a major fortification. The enormous enclosure, divided into four wards, is nearly 1000 feet long, and it occupies a natural plateau surrounded by cliffs and a ravine, except on the east side where the artificial defences are supplemented by a wet moat.

BARNARD CASTLE
Co. Durham
OS 92 NZ 049165
Barnard Castle stands near the centre of the town of the same name, which is sixteen miles west of Darlington, via the A67: it can also be reached from the main A1 trunk road, by turning west at Scotch Corner and travelling via the A66 and the B6277. Nearby are the notable ruins of Egglestone Abbey; and the Bowes Museum, in its palatial Victorian country house.

Barnard Castle's formidable ditch and curtain wall.

Traditionally, it is believed that Battle Abbey was founded as a result of a vow made by William before the Battle of Hastings, in which he promised to build a monastery on the site, if he was granted victory over King Harold and the Saxons. Four monks from the Benedictine abbey of Marmoutier, on the Loire, came from France to form the nucleus of the new abbey's community, and the high altar of the abbey church was built on the very spot where Harold had been killed. As the French monks lacked financial resources, the king's treasury funded all the building costs, and by 1076 the eastern end of the abbey church was sufficiently advanced to allow the building to be used. In February 1094 the abbey church was finally finished and consecrated in the presence of William II and the Archbishop of Canterbury. On his death-bed William the Conqueror endowed the abbey with so much land and wealth that it became one of the wealthiest monasteries in England.

Little remains of the Norman abbey, but traces of late eleventh or early twelfth century masonry can be seen in a house attached to the magnificent fourteenth century gatehouse, as well as in the outline of the abbey church and the footings of the recently excavated chapter house. The main ruins date from the thirteenth and fourteenth centuries.
See **The Battle of Hastings.**

BATTLE ABBEY East Sussex
OS 199 TQ 748156
Battle Abbey and town are seven miles north-west of Hastings, via the A2100: and the famous battle site of 1066, immediately adjacent to the abbey ruins, is well worth a visit.

13

Here stood Battle Abbey's high altar, marking the spot where King Harold fell during the battle of Hastings.

BERKHAMSTED Hertfordshire
OS 165 SP 995082
*Berkhamsted Castle stands to the
north of Berkhamsted town, which is
twenty-eight miles north-west of
central London, via the A41(T).*

The most outstanding feature of this now-ruined castle are its earthworks, built on a substantial scale. The motte is forty-five feet high, and 180 feet in diameter at its base. It stands at the north-east corner of the large bailey, itself 300 by 450 feet and surrounded by a wide, water-filled ditch. It is probable that the original motte and bailey castle was built not long after the Conquest, when Berkhamsted was given by William to his half-brother Robert, Count of Mortain. Berkhamsted lay on the circuitous route which William took on his way from the Battle of Hastings to the eventual surrender of London in December 1066.

On the north and east are a series of outer earthworks, consisting of a high bank against which are built a number of external bastions. The dating of these is in doubt, and they have been variously interpreted as platforms for medieval siege engines or Civil War defences. They have been badly damaged by road and railway building.

On top of the motte are the ruins of a circular keep and a well, and parts of a staircase and fireplace are visible. Two wing walls run up the motte to the keep, and around the bailey are the badly robbed remains of the curtain wall and half round towers. It is difficult to interpret the fragmentary masonry, but the oldest remains probably date from 1155–65, when the king's 'houses' on the motte are mentioned. The castle, having had a great number of owners, fell into disrepair in the fourteenth century and it was probably not inhabited after 1495.

Trees now grow on Berkhamsted Castle's great motte.

14

The church is all that survives of a once massive Benedictine priory, founded in 1088 by Robert de Busli, lord of Tickhill, and linked to St Catherine's Priory at Rouen in Normandy. Even here much of the original Norman work has been destroyed and, to further complicate the picture, the church has received a number of additions through the ages. The large south aisle was added in c.1300. Some two hundred years later the fine Perpendicular tower, complete with pinnacles and bell-openings, was built: and in the late seventeenth century the incongruous east wall was added in a classical style. All this has to be mentally discarded to visualize the building as it was erected within a generation of the Conquest.

Norman work of the 1090s is to be found in the nave and the north aisle. The gallery and clerestory are typical of many important Norman churches. Particular attention should be paid to the rubble-work walls which are very thick with roughly-dressed stone; to the thick mortar joints; and the simple sculpting of the capitals. Compare all this with the well-dressed blocks and the carving in the fourteenth century south aisle. Yet ashlar masonry of this latter quality was already being erected in the 1090s, and one of the main interests of this site is the use made by its builders of obsolete techniques.

BLYTH PRIORY
Nottinghamshire
OS 120 SK 625873

The priory is in the centre of Blyth, which is seven miles north-east of Worksop and twelve miles south of Doncaster. The village, dominated by the priory church tower, is less than a mile west of the main A1 trunk road, from which it is signposted: indeed, the priory once derived some of its revenues from tolls levied on travellers and thus, according to legend, fell foul of the local outlaw Robin Hood.

The baroque cherubs on Blyth's seventeenth-century font counterpoint the severity of the priory's soaring early Norman arches.

The Normans

During the second half of the eleventh century, men from a single province in northern France conquered not only England, but also southern Italy and Sicily: and came near to conquering not only Scotland and Wales but also Spain, at one stage threatening even the great Byzantine empire of Constantinople. Nor were their exploits confined by the bounds of Europe, for they played a leading part in the capture of Jerusalem during the First Crusade; established a principality based on Antioch in Syria; and for a time occupied part of North Africa

These remarkable men were, of course, the Normans: and though by 1066 they proudly called themselves "Frenchmen" or "Franks", their more familiar name proclaims that they were not originally of French ancestry. The Normans, in fact, had begun as "northmen" or "norsemen", an eddy of the great wave of Viking raiders who terrorised Christian Europe during the ninth century: and while their fellow-pirates were ravaging and all but overwhelming Anglo-Saxon England, the first Normans were sailing up the Seine to attack Paris. In France, as in England, the Viking onslaught was eventually checked, if only by allowing the raiders to occupy and settle specific areas of land. And thus, in 911, a defeated but still formidable Scandinavian chieftain named Rolf was permitted by the Frankish Emperor Charles III to settle with his followers in the lower Seine valley, he undertaking in return to accept baptism as a Christian. This Rolf was the great-great-great-grandfather of William the Conqueror: and the "lands of the northmen" he was granted – subsequently much expanded by his son William Longsword – became the Duchy of Normandy.

The process by which Normandy and the Normans were gradually absorbed into the mainstream of Frankish culture is far from clear. It seems plain, however, that the settlers were essentially a warrior hierarchy superimposed onto a French-speaking peasant population, and by about 1025 their Scandinavian language had already died out in many parts of Normandy. The newcomers, too, inter-married readily with the natives, while their Dukes – probably as a matter of policy – invariably chose marriage alliances with non-Scandinavian brides. It is equally evident, moreover, that the northmen took over the administrative institutions of their lands – which had previously been the Frankish kingdom of Neustria, and before that the Roman province based on Rouen – more or less unaltered: and that after a few relapses into paganism they not only embraced Christianity but also – with the help of the church reformers encouraged by the Conqueror's grandfather, Duke Richard II – created a Norman church with a formidable reputation for efficiency and scholarship. Long before 1066, in short, the norsemen had become Normans, effectively French in their language, law, culture and political ideals.

All the same, they neither entirely forgot their Scandinavian origins nor abandoned their concept of themselves as a distinct (and a distinctly superior) people. Many of the Conqueror's contemporaries, for example, bore Christian names – Osbern, Turketil or Ranulf – with a decidedly Scandinavian ring: while the Norman love of not always flattering nicknames – Robert the Weasel and Roger Moneybags, Herbert Wake-Dog and Robert Curthose ("short stockings") – may likewise have been inherited from their Viking forbears. Such Norman nicknames, incidentally, still survive as English surnames like Russell ("red-headed"), Gulliver (*goulafre*, "glutton"), Pettifer (*pied-de-fer*, "ironfoot") and Pauncefoot ("round-belly"). From the Vikings, too, the Normans perhaps derived their notorious greed and ruthlessness; their ability to adapt themselves to almost any situation; and their willingness to learn from and use men of other nations when it suited them. The "Norman" Archbishops Lanfranc and Anselm of Canterbury, for instance, were Italian; the cathedral-building Bishop Losinga of Norwich was a Lorrainer; while several of the greatest landowners in post-Conquest England were Bretons.

Such characteristics, if scarcely endearing, were of great assistance to the Normans during their remarkable career of conquest. Rather less so, however, was their tendency to extreme individualism and unruliness: for, as one of their own chroniclers admitted, "the Normans are a turbulent people . . . ever ready for mischief. When under the rule of a strong master, they are a most valiant race . . . but in all other circumstances they will soon turn and rend each other, bringing ruin on their own heads". During much of its early history, indeed, Normandy was riven by feud and civil war: and it was not until (by about 1054) William the Conqueror had finally brought it under firm control, establishing a strong state backed by a united baronage and a reformed church, that the Duchy really began to influence the affairs of Europe.

The instruments by which it did so, of course, were its soldiers. For the Normans, like their Viking progenitors, were first and foremost warriors: though unlike the Vikings (and unlike the English they defeated at Hastings) they had long since abandoned the old Germanic tradition of fighting on foot, in favour of the Frankish mode of mounted warfare. They became, in fact, the most feared and formidable horsemen in Europe. Riding fierce and well-trained warhorses, and fully equipped with conical helmet, long coat of mail, kite-shaped shield, heavy sword and long lance, their most devastating tactic was the cavalry charge: which one Byzantine writer believed to be so utterly irresistible that "it would punch a hole in the very walls of Babylon". Neither were they behindhand in cunning, and at Hastings and elsewhere they employed the favourite Norse stratagem of the "feigned flight", luring the enemy into disorderly pursuit and then turning to hack them pieces. They were famous, too, for their highly efficient military organisation – well illustrated by the Bayeux Tapestry's scenes of the building and provisioning of Duke William's invasion fleet: and no less so for their use of the castle, at first as a campaign base in hostile territory and later to hold down conquered lands.

Despite all their cunning and efficiency, despite their ruthlessness and skill in war and statecraft, and despite their amazing achievements between 1050 and 1100, the Normans were not to endure long as a distinct political force: and within two centuries of Hastings they had been all but absorbed into the lands they conquered, with Normandy itself firmly back under the control of the kings of France. Yet in England, at least, these extraordinary Normans left their indelible mark on the state, on society, and on the landscape itself.

See **William the Conqueror; Castles of the Norman Conquest.**

BOOTHBY PAGNELL
MANOR HOUSE Lincolnshire
OS 130 SK 971307

The Norman manor house, not always open to the public, stands in the grounds of the much later Boothby Pagnell Hall, on the outskirts of the village. Boothby Pagnell village is five miles south-east of Grantham and four miles east of the main A1 road (from which it is signposted) via a minor road through Great Ponton, whose splendid late medieval church tower is noteworthy.

This manor house, built in about 1200, represents a very pleasing and largely original example of its type. It consists of a two storey building with a hall and solar over vaulted undercrofts. It is quite small, measuring some fifty feet by twenty-six feet overall. The solar (or private room) is built in one unit with the hall and has a good Norman window, with two round-headed lights crowned by a tympanum. The roof is post-medieval (the original would have been much steeper-pitched).

It is not known who was responsible for building the manor house, but it was clearly a local family of some substance. The erection of such houses marked the beginning of the movement away from fortified castles into more luxurious residences.

See **Burton Agnes Old Hall and Church.**

Raised above ground level for security, the entrance to Boothby Pagnell manor house led directly into the hall on the upper floor. Apply to the Hall for permission to view.

The red sandstone ruins of the castle stand in a beautiful setting on the south bank of the River Eamont, just above the floodplain. Long before the Normans came, however, this site had been of strategic importance to the Romans as the focus of a network of roads. A fort guarded the river crossing, and an extensive civil settlement grew up around it. The earthworks of the unexcavated fort may still be seen to the south of the castle.

Several centuries later Brougham marked the north-western limit of a tract of land stretching from the River Eamont to Stainmore, called Westmorland. In the eleventh and twelfth centuries this land oscillated between English and Scottish control until Henry II finally brought the area firmly under the English crown. The earliest part of the stone castle is the square keep built towards the end of Henry's reign in c.1180, when it clearly formed an important stronghold against the Scots. It is presumed that the other contemporary buildings were of wood, and it has been suggested that the Roman fort may well have served as an outer bailey at this period.

In the thirteenth century the castle was inherited by the Clifford family, who also controlled three other important castles in the area: Appleby, Brough and Pendragon. At that time the curtain wall and further accommodation and domestic buildings were added. The keep was heightened and connected to the external defences by an inner gatehouse, and when the outer gatehouse was added in the fourteenth century, the whole made an impressive military gate-defence with secure and comfortable living quarters, comparable to Dunstanburgh on the eastern seaboard.

After the Cliffords' downfall during the Wars of the Roses, the stronghold lost its strategic importance and was neglected until the seventeenth century: when a successor, Lady Anne Clifford, undertook a vast restoration programme. Following this short period of respite, however, Brougham was again abandoned, stripped of its lead and timber and left to decay.

Opposite, the Norman keep and later gatehouse of Brougham Castle stand on the site of a Roman fort.

BROUGHAM CASTLE
Cumbria
OS 90 NY 532290
The castle stands just by the A66 road from Penrith to Appleby, two miles south-east of Penrith and junction 40 of the M6 motorway.

Buildwas Abbey lies on the southern bank of the River Severn, just before the river enters the Ironbridge Gorge. The house was founded from Savigny in 1135 but, like its sisters, became attached to the Cistercian order in 1147. The abbey plan has been adapted from the normal Cistercian layout to accommodate its location on a narrow river plateau. The cloister was sited to the north of the church in order to obtain adequate drainage, but otherwise the arrangement of buildings was normal. The surviving abbey ruins are regarded as a fine example of Norman transitional architecture, dating from the period between 1160 and 1200. Only the shell of the church survives, together with the east range of the cloister buildings, but its wooded location gives it charm and tranquility and provides a dramatic contrast with the nearby remnants of the Industrial Revolution. The late medieval monks of Buildwas, nevertheless, can possibly be identified as the earliest iron masters on the Shropshire coalfield.

BUILDWAS ABBEY
Shropshire
OS 127 SJ 643043
The abbey is about five miles south of the new town of Telford, on the B4380 from Shrewsbury and Wroxeter to Ironbridge: it can also be reached from Much Wenlock, via the B4378. Nearby is the fascinating Ironbridge Gorge Museum.

The mightly pillars of Buildwas Abbey's ruined nave display the solid strength inherent in Norman architecture.

The crypt beneath the east range of Buildwas Abbey's monastic buildings still has some of its original flooring.

The Norman Old Hall, the 'new' Jacobean Hall, and the church of St Martin form a fine group in this picturesque village.

The late Norman manor house known as the Old Hall is something of a surprise, for from the outside it has the appearance of a Georgian brick house. Its Norman stonework is concealed on all sides, except the west, by a brick skin. During the eighteenth century, the Old Hall (which was replaced by the New Hall of Sir Henry Griffiths, c.1601–12) was thus disguised and used as a laundry.

The Norman manor house is a first floor hall, a type of house popular with the late Norman aristocracy, and was built in c.1170–80 by Roger de Stuteville. The hall stands over a basement or cellar which is divided into two aisles by a row of three cylindrical columns. Access between this and the first-floor hall was by means of a newel or spiral staircase in the north-west corner of the building. The walls are a solid five feet thick. The large windows on the first floor are a later addition. This is one of only twenty or so late Norman domestic buildings to survive in the country.

To the west lies the church of St Martin with a number of Norman features, notably the chancel arch and the fine drum-shaped font with blank arcading around it.
See **Boothby Pagnell.**

BURTON AGNES Humberside
OS 101 TA 102633
Burton Agnes village is near the east coast of Yorkshire, six miles west of Bridlington on the A166. The halls and church stand together near the village duckpond, and the Old Hall (signposted) and church are open all the year round. The "new" Jacobean Hall, notable for its interiors and "Screaming Skull" legend, is open during spring and summer, and well worth visiting.

BURY ST EDMUNDS Suffolk
OS 155 TL 856650
Bury St Edmunds, one of the most interesting towns in East Anglia, is twenty-eight miles east of Cambridge via the A45(T). The monastic buildings are near the town centre, off Abbeygate Street, and Moyses Hall is not far away, on Cornhill.

This imposing Norman gatehouse is one of the few surviving relics of the once-great abbey at Bury St. Edmunds.

Bury St Edmunds developed as a great monastic centre after the bones of St Edmund, King and Martyr, were brought here in 908. The Domesday Book (1086) records a new town in the process of being laid out to the west of the abbey precinct, in an area which included former arable land. Of the Norman abbey church no more than large fragments of flint rubble remain, together with outlines of the walls, now located in a public park. Of the associated monastic buildings the chief Norman monument is the southern gatehouse, dated 1120–48, which serves as a bell-tower for St James's church. This tall and imposing building, four storeys high, combines castle-like strength with elaborate external decoration. On the ground floor a wide entrance arch, projecting like a porch, is surmounted by a pointed gable covered in fish-scale carving: and above this – on all four sides of the tower – rise tier upon tier of round-arched windows. Elsewhere in the town, in the market place, is Moyses Hall, a two storied Norman stone house dated about 1180: this has round arches and windows, and a hall and solar on the upper level.

CAMBRIDGE Cambridgeshire
OS 154 TL 449588
*Cambridge is sixty miles north of
London, via the M11 motorway. Holy
Sepulchre church (also called "the
Round Church") is on Bridge Street,
to the north of the town centre area.*

Despite its wealth of medieval and later archi-tecture, Cambridge contains relatively little from the Norman era. It does however have one gem, the church of the Holy Sepulchre in Bridge Street. This was built by the Fraternity of the Holy Sepulchre in about 1130, on the model of the church of the Holy Sepulchre in Jerusalem. Its circular nave was characteristic of Knights Templar churches, of which only a few survive in this country. It has short round piers and a galleried and ribbed dome, as well as a rib vaulted ambulatory or processional walkway around it. It was restored by Anthony Salvin in 1841, who also added a Gothic oblong chancel. *See* **Ludlow.**

CARISBROOKE CASTLE
Isle of Wight
OS 196 SZ 488878
*The castle is to the south of
Carisbrooke, which is near the centre
of the Isle of Wight and just over a
mile south-west of Newport, via the
B3401.*

A motte and bailey castle was established here shortly after the Conquest by William Fitz-Osbern. Carisbrooke is the only notable fortification in the Isle of Wight, and is also one of the earliest known castle conversions from timber to stone.

A Norman shell keep sits on the motte, and within the keep is a well 160 feet deep. There is also a continuous Norman curtain wall which appears to follow the circuit of a Roman fort: and immediately north of the gatehouse, within the curtain wall, is a rare twelfth century garderobe, or lavatory.

The domestic buildings and chapel within the bailey are mostly of the sixteenth century, but the fabric of the great hall dates from the twelfth century.

The curtain wall of Carisbrooke Castle follows the outline of Roman fort defences.

This stone shell keep replaced the wooden-stake palisade which originally crowned Carisbrooke's huge earthen motte. Within the keep, and vital in times of siege, is a 160 foot deep well plunging down through the mound.

Medieval and modern Carlisle stand on the site of the important Roman settlement of *Luguvalium*. When the Norman city walls were built between 1092 and the late twelfth century, they used Roman building stone, and enclosed much of the former Roman town. Carlisle castle is a classic Norman motte and bailey, situated close to the river Eden, with inner and outer baileys and moats. The town developed to the south of the castle, whose plan is basically unchanged today, although the stone keep is the only surviving Norman building.

In 1092 William Rufus captured Carlisle from the Scots, and his first castle was probably of earth and timber. It was taken by the Scots again in 1135 but they restored it to Henry II in 1157, at which time the defences were considerably strengthened with a stone keep and curtain wall. The castle was used throughout the Middle Ages and also under Henry VIII, and many of the buildings were repaired and rebuilt many times.

In about c.1102 Henry I granted a site at Carlisle for the foundation of a religious establishment, and in the 1120s he established a community of Augustinian canons regular here: their red sandstone church, which was to become the cathedral, was already under construction by 1130. Then, in 1133, in an attempt to secure this area for the English rather than the Scottish crown, Henry made Carlisle a cathedral city.

The buildings which survive in the abbey precinct are predominantly sixteenth century or later, but there are parts of the original Norman work in the cathedral. These include two of the original eight bays of the nave, the crossing, and the south transept. The nave pillars are massive, round and plain with simply decorated cushion capitals, and some of the arches have a simple incised chevron motif. As you come in through the south door, you will notice the extraordinary subsidence in the Norman structure: on the arches you can see that there is up to twelve inches difference in height between the column capitals!

CARLISLE Cumbria
OS 85 NY 396564
Carlisle, reached via the M6, is three hundred miles north of London and about a hundred miles south of Edinburgh. The cathedral is near the town centre and the railway station, and the castle somewhat to the north.

Carlisle's squat Norman keep.

23

Henry of Blois: Twelfth Century Prince Bishop

Few Norman bishops have left such a legacy of standing remains and sculpture as has Henry of Blois, Bishop of Winchester between 1129 and 1171. He was more of a princely baron than a Christian bishop, for not only was he a statesman but also a king-maker and a member of the royal family. His was one of the most striking episcopates in Winchester Cathedral's history, and he spent much of his income on the building of castles and palaces, although in the later years of his episcopy he became much more of an energetic ecclesiastic and a lavish patron of the arts.

He was the fourth son of Adela, the daughter of William the Conqueror, and of Stephen, Count of Blois and Chartres. The date of his birth is, however, not clear. Since his father was already dead in 1102 and Henry was not the youngest child he must have been born in the 1090's or earlier. While his brother Stephen, later King of England, was sent to be educated by their maternal uncle Henry I, Henry of Blois was sent to become a monk at the famous monastery at Cluny, near Dijon in France. In 1126, when he finally arrived in England, Henry I made Henry of Blois Abbot of Glastonbury, the richest and one of the oldest abbeys in England. At Glastonbury, Henry completed the work started by his predecessors Abbots Herluin and Pelochin: namely the construction of a larger church, the re-building of a palace and an abbey gateway and the reconstruction of the cloister, refectory and other domestic buildings. He also added a bell tower to the church. Many of these buildings were, however, destroyed by fire in 1184.

In 1129 Henry I made Henry of Blois Bishop of Winchester, a position second only to Canterbury in power and wealth. Until the 1180s Winchester, the ancient capital of England, surpassed even Westminster in importance, since it was the seat of the royal treasury. This was an important factor which led to Henry becoming an important ecclesiastical magnate in the middle years of the twelfth century. He was both Bishop of Winchester and Abbot of Glastonbury until his death in August 1171. Because of his influence at both the royal court and the papal court in Rome, Henry was chiefly responsible for his brother Stephen's succession to the English throne in 1135.

Soon after the death of Henry I, Henry of Blois secured the government for his brother Stephen by obtaining the support of three important statesmen. These were the Bishop of Salisbury, Henry I's chief justiciar and most trusted friend William Pont de l'Arche; the sheriff of Hampshire and Wiltshire and the custodian of the castle at Winchester where the royal treasury was kept; and the Archbishop of Canterbury, William de Corbeil, whose support was required to crown the new king of England, which he did three days before Christmas 1135.

Behind Henry of Blois' king-making activities, however, lay a motive. He wished to secure the freedom and liberty of the Church from royal control and interference. Consequently in 1136 Stephen co-operated by issuing a charter which gave Henry exactly what he wanted. Nevertheless two years later Stephen was in conflict with his bishop brother, who after the death of William de Corbeil in 1136 strongly desired to be elected Archbishop of Canterbury. However, Stephen took a hand in the election of the new prelate and Theobald of Bec became archbishop. Not only did Henry thus lose face over the appointment, but he also lost his position as first advisor to the king and the consequent influence in the elevation to high office of men who were opposed to his policies. Consequently Henry openly took sides with Stephen's rival for the throne – the Empress Matilda, Henry I's daughter.

In 1139 Stephen took an even more active hand in removing obstacles in his way by capturing the Bishop of Salisbury and two other powerful statesmen who were controlling central government in England. These events, along with the Empress Matilda's hereditary claim to the throne, sparked off the civil war which troubled England for nearly twenty years, until Stephen's death in 1154.

It was during this early period in Henry of Blois' episcopate (1129–1138) that he built (or rebuilt) palaces and castles, founded two religious establishments and rebuilt much of Romsey Abbey.

Documentary sources record that between 1129 and 1138 the Bishop of Winchester built castles at Farnham, Taunton, Downton in Wiltshire, and Merdon, near Winchester; and palaces at Wolvesey in Winchester and at Bishop's Waltham, also in Hampshire. With the exception of Downton all these buildings have left substantial remains.

Between 1132 and 1137 Henry also founded the Hospital of St. Cross for the Knights Templars, in the meadows near the banks of the river Itchen on the southern outskirts of Winchester. Also around the same time he founded a college of canons at Marwell, a rural manor which lay on the road between his palaces at Wolvesey and Bishop's Waltham. In Winchester, within a few years of Stephen's succession, Henry of Blois was in control not only of his rebuilt palace at Wolvesey but also of the royal castle, the royal treasury and perhaps also the royal palace. He surrendered both the castle and the king's treasure to Matilda in March 1141, after an abortive attempt to negotiate a compromise peace between his brother and Matilda in the previous year. The Empress, however, also broke her promises to Henry and as a result, within a few months, the bishop withdrew his support from her and once more transferred his allegiance to Stephen. After Henry's change of sides Matilda besieged Winchester in July 1141 and Henry retaliated. His forces burnt the city together with most of the churches, St. Mary's Abbey, Hyde Abbey and possibly the royal palace. Stephen sent troops to assist Henry and Matilda was put to flight. After this event Henry and the city remained on Stephen's side.

In 1142 Henry helped his brother fortify a castle at Wilton in Wiltshire, in order to block the route from the west, where the Empress's principal supporters were based. Throughout these events Henry attempted to bring about an alliance between Church and King and he tried, but failed, to persuade the Pope to elevate Winchester into an archbishopric in order to rival the metropolitan see of Canterbury.

In 1150, Henry Plantagenet, Duke of Normandy and son of the Empress Matilda and Geoffrey Plantagenet, was gaining support as the rightful heir to the English throne. By this time England was tired of the long-drawn-out civil war and so it was time to negotiate peace. As a result of Henry of Blois' intrigues, late in 1153 Stephen and Duke Henry met at Winchester for a final reconciliation. The next year Stephen died, Duke Henry became King Henry II, and with his accession the civil war finally ended.

These events signified a turning point in Henry of Blois's career. Fearing that the new king would seek revenge for his desertion of Empress Matilda in 1141, Henry of Blois fled from England and sought asylum at his old school, the monastery at Cluny. However, after being assured of his safety in England, the bishop returned to his see at Winchester.

Subsequently Henry avoided the political arena: and the remaining years of his life were dedicated to ecclesiastical building, works of devotion, and the patronage of art. Although he did not greatly contribute to the fabric of Winchester cathedral, he was active in other ways such as the translation of relics and the enlargement of the cathedral treasury. His gifts to the cathedral included fine metalwork, enamels, hangings, vestments and books. He commissioned the illuminated Winchester Psalter for his personal use, while the major part of the great Winchester Bible was probably completed during his bishopric.

Bishop Henry was also interested in estate management, and as Abbot of Glastonbury and Bishop of Winchester kept records of the various properties and estates of both houses. In 1148 he undertook a detailed survey of Winchester known as the *Winton Domesday*, and he may have even been responsible for commissioning the great cathedral record, the *Codex Wintoniensis*. Whilst in exile at Cluny in the late 1150's, Henry also appears to have made a survey of that abbey's rents and thus rescued the abbey from bankruptcy.

Henry of Blois also provided some of his rural manors with sculptures for their churches and was probably responsible for rebuilding a number of his manor houses in stone: as at Rookwood, near Hambledon, in Hampshire, and at Alverstoke and East Meon, in the same county. Four of the eight black Tournai marble founts in England are in Hampshire churches, (Winchester Cathedral, East Meon church, St. Michael's Southampton and at the parish church at St. Mary Bourne), and are thought to have been Henry's gifts sometime in the 1150s. Perhaps these good works in his later years, in art and the welfare of his diocese, were by way of penance for his earlier ambitious and political scheming. Henry of Blois, Prince Bishop, died peacefully aged at least 80 in August 1171.

In 1190 William Marshall founded a house of Augustinian regular canons here. The area is thought to have been totally uninhabited at that time, and the church took over a century to build. The first brethren came from Bradenstoke Priory in Wiltshire and were granted extensive lands in the valley, together with possessions in Ireland.

Although initially there were twelve canons and a prior here, by the sixteenth century the community was considerably smaller. The earliest parts of the church, (including the transepts, crossing, choir and part of the unusually short nave) are transitional Norman; and the richly carved south doorway dates from c.1200. In the fifteenth century,

probably because the ground was unstable, the monastic buildings were moved from the south of the church to the north: the former doorway to the dormitory can still be seen in the south transept, together with some corbels of the cloister roof, and part of the cloister bench.

The priory was dissolved in 1537, and although the monastic buildings no longer survive, the picturesque predominantly fourteenth century gatehouse may still be seen in the village square, while the line of the precinct wall of the priory exists in property and field boundaries. The church was subsequently used as the parish church and has therefore survived relatively intact.

CARTMEL PRIORY Cumbria
OS 96 SD 379788
Cartmel is six miles east of Ulverston and two miles west of Grange-over-Sands, on the north shore of Morecambe Bay: it can be reached from junction 36 of the M6 via the A6 and the A590, turning south-west on minor roads in the Lindale area. The church and abbey gatehouse are in the centre of the attractive village.

CASTLE ACRE Norfolk
OS 132 TF 813148
Castle Acre is twelve miles east of King's Lynn and four miles north of Swaffham, via the A1065. The priory is just south of the village, and is signposted

Gracefully intersecting arches, as seen here at Castle Acre Priory, are a characteristically Norman decorative motif.

Castle Acre Priory was a Cluniac foundation, lying in the valley of the Nar. It was founded in c.1090 by William, second Earl of Warenne, whose father had introduced the Cluniac monks into England at Lewes. The original scheme here was that the monks should form part of the population of the new castle (as at Old Sarum) but this concept soon proved unworkable, and a site was given to the monks a little to the west. The original Norman church was never rebuilt and the west front, even in its ruined state, represents one of the most graceful monuments of its age. The remainder of the ruined buildings

follow the normal monastic scheme, and overall Castle Acre provides one of the most impressive, virtually complete, Norman monastic ruins in southern Britain.

The castle consists of a fine late twelfth century stone shell keep sitting on the earthworks of an earlier motte and bailey castle. Recent excavations have revealed an unusual building dating from about 1080, which resembles later fortified manor houses rather than contemporary castle constructions. In addition to the castle, evidence of Norman town defences in the form of earthworks still dominate the topography of Castle Acre.

The superb west front of Castle Acre Priory; and details from its interior, with a spiral carved column.

The quiet and pleasant village of Castle Rising, once a port but now several miles from the marshy coastline of the Wash, has two splendid relics of our Norman past, the castle and the church of St Lawrence.

The castle, built by William de Albini on the site of an earlier village and church, dates from the "Anarchy" of the 1130s. This was a period when the Crown temporarily lost control over castle-building and noblemen everywhere were able to erect "adulterine" castles as a direct challenge to royal authority. Many were simple earth and timber fortifications, rather like those built immediately after the Conquest, but that at Castle Rising was more substantial. Although now in ruins, enough survives to show that de Albini's castle was in many ways ahead of its time in terms of domestic comfort. The main building was the palatial hall-keep, entered through a forebuilding and with its principal living quarters on the first floor. These comprised a hall and chamber (each with its own pair of garde-robes, thought to be among the earliest examples of "ladies" and "gents" lavatories in the country), a kitchen with service room west of the hall, and a chapel at the east end of the chamber.

Defensive considerations were undoubtedly secondary. Although the castle was capable of withstanding a siege (albeit never put to this test) de Albini's main intention at Castle Rising was to erect a building, more of a palace than a fortress, which was worthy of his status and aspirations. To this end he lavished money on the external decoration of the castle, particularly the rich blank arcading on the forebuilding, and in providing every comfort for his new wife, Henry I's widow. Such indeed was the emphasis on domestic luxury and display, that by the end of the century (following the strengthening of the ramparts and the completion of the outer fortifications) the keep was defensively obsolete except as an ultimate place of refuge.

Remains of the original church can be seen embedded in the late twelfth century rampart north of the keep, but a new church on a new site was built by de Albini. Despite considerable restoration in the mid-nineteenth century, it is still a good example of a large twelfth century church with a central tower. The west front and the elaborately carved west crossing arch inside are particularly impressive.

CASTLE RISING Norfolk
OS 132 TF 666246
Castle Rising is four miles north-east of King's Lynn, just west of the A149.

Inside the forebuilding of de Albini's sumptuous keep at Castle Rising.

29

CHARNEY BASSET
Oxfordshire
OS 165 SU 380945

Charney Basset is four miles north-west of Wantage and fourteen miles south-west of Oxford: it can be reached by turning south off the A420 Oxford-Faringdon road, just west of Kingston Bagpuize. Note also the rare medieval wooden pulpit in the church.

The small church of St Peter stands close to the manor house. Its principal feature of interest is the well preserved Norman doorway on the south side. There is a fine outer moulding to the door-arch, with carved radially set faces, their tongues out and fork-like beards on their chins. Inside is a remarkable eleventh century tympanum now set into the north wall of the chancel. The central figure is of a standing man holding two griffins and apparently being bitten by them! It is possible that this scene illustrates the legendary Flight of Alexander the Great, being borne up to heaven by griffins. The church was given to Abingdon Priory by Ralph Bassett in about 1120, and this might explain the use of such obscure imagery.

The mysterious 'griffin' tympanum at Charney Basset.

CHEPSTOW CASTLE Gwent
OS 162 ST 533941

The castle, set on a towering rock above the River Wye, dominates the town: this stands at the northern, Welsh, end of the Severn Bridge, and is reached via junction 22 of the M4 from Bristol to Cardiff. Alternatively, it can be reached from Monmouth via the picturesque Wye Valley road, the A466.

Chepstow is a spectacular introduction to Wales and the Welsh Marches. The castle commands a strong defensive position on a narrow spur of rock which runs eastwards between the River Wye and a deep ravine. Chepstow (or "Striguil" as it was known) is a fine example of Norman castle building. The rectangular keep straddles the entire width of the rocky spur, with an upper bailey and barbican to the west and a middle and lower bailey to the east. The keep, which incidentally possesses the earliest datable tympanum in the British Isles, was begun in c.1070 by the great Marcher lord William Fitz-Osbern, a friend and close adviser of William the Conqueror. The upper and lower baileys date from the thirteenth century and were constructed during the lordships of William Marshall and of Hugh Bigod. A large mural tower to the south-east of the twin towered gatehouse of the lower bailey, known as Marten's Tower, was also constructed during Hugh Bigod's lordship. In the thirteenth century, the original eleventh century keep was heightened and enlarged to enhance its domestic accommodation, proving that the keep was still favoured as the ultimate stronghold and symbol of lordship. Elsewhere contemporary thirteenth century trends brought about a move to the gatehouse as the ultimate strongpoint, but at Chepstow the old Norman tradition was adhered to.

A house of secular canons was established here in about 907, dedicated to St Werburgh, the seventh century Mercian saint, whose relics had been brought from Hanbury (Staffordshire) to Chester in about 875. In 1092, however, as part of the Norman reform of the English church, it was re-founded by Hugh Lupus, second Earl of Chester, as a Benedictine abbey. He was helped by Anselm of Bec, who in the following year was to become Archbishop of Canterbury as successor to Lanfranc.

Characteristically, the re-founding of the community was accompanied by a systematic programme of rebuilding, and therefore no traces remain of the pre-Conquest buildings. By contrast with St Albans, no use seems to have been made of Roman building materials, which considering Chester originated as the Roman city of *Deva*, is somewhat surprising. Instead the new abbey was constructed almost entirely of red sandstone. The most impressive survival from this church is the north transept, with its great round-headed arch. This originally led into a semi-circular chapel to the east, the foundations of which can still be seen in the floor of the present early thirteenth century chapel. Otherwise the only relic of Earl Hugh's building is the north wall of the north aisle, doubling as the south wall of the cloister, which survived the reconstruction of the latter in 1525–30.

It seems that western towers, similar to those at Southwell (Nottinghamshire), were also originally intended; but now all that remains is some stonework dating from around 1140 at the north-west corner of the nave. Behind the magnificent late fourteenth century choir stalls, the floor has been cut away to reveal the circular base of one of the pillars of the Norman choir. Of the original monastic buildings, only the early twelfth century groin-vaulted undercroft in the west claustral range, where the cellarer kept the abbey's provisions, survives. Above this were the abbot's lodgings (now demolished) and the so-called Anselm's chapel, built in the twelfth century but extensively re-modelled in the reign of Charles I. Like other monasteries, the abbey was dissolved by Henry VIII in 1540: but in the following year the church became the cathedral of the new diocese of Chester.

CHESTER CATHEDRAL
Cheshire
OS 117 SJ 406665
Chester, thirty-eight miles south-west of Manchester, is best reached via the M6 and M56 motorways. The cathedral is in the centre of this most attractive and interesting city, off Eastgate Street: and visitors should also see the two miles of medieval city walls and the well-known (if much-restored) "Rows" of two-storied shops. St John's church has a fine Norman nave and crossing.

CHRISTCHURCH Dorset
OS 195 SZ 159925
Christchurch is on the coast, immediately east of Bournemouth on the A35. The splendid church is also famous for its late medieval tombs and the carved misericords beneath the choir stalls.

The magnificent Norman nave of Christchurch Priory, with its three storeys of arches – arcade, gallery, and clerestory – rising one above the other: beyond the screen is the later medieval choir of this longest of all English parish churches.

The town was originally known as Twineham, but now takes its name from the priory church, which has become the longest parish church in England (312 feet). The present church occupies the site of a Saxon foundation, which apparently went back as far as the seventh century. It was Ranulf Flambard, dean under William Rufus, who initiated the

31

building of the Norman church (much larger than its predecessor) of which parts survive today. Flambard left in 1099 to become Bishop of Durham, and was disgraced a year later, after King William's death, so that the building he began was not finished until 1150. The church originally had a semi-circular eastern end, and a central tower. The former feature has disappeared, while the tower was rebuilt after collapsing in the fourteenth century. What remains of the Norman church is the nave and the crossing beneath the tower. The nave pillars and the arcading above are absolutely superb, while the central crossing displays some wonderful decorative detail. From the outside it is the transepts which are

most noticeably Norman, the northern one being particularly spectacular, with a remarkable stair turret at its eastern corner. Traces of two Norman windows may be seen in the southern transept. Little remains of Christchurch's Norman castle, which was ruined in the Civil War, but a climb up the motte is rewarded by a fine view. The keep is now a shell, although it does have some Norman characteristics. The inner ward now serves as a bowling green, to one side of which are the remains of the twelfth century hall with fine Norman windows and chimney.

Elaborately carved columns, intersecting arches, and "fish-scale" patterned stone decorate this Norman stair turret at Christchurch Priory.

Picturesquely sited in the Clun Valley amid the rolling south-west Shropshire hills, the little town of Clun – along with its neighbours Clunton, Clunbury and Clungunford – was said by the poet Housman to be among "the quietest places under the sun". But it was not always so, for this is Welsh border country, and a motte and bailey castle was most probably built here soon after the Norman Conquest. Certainly Clun Castle was besieged and burnt by the Welsh Lord Rhys in 1196, and it was perhaps after this that a much more formidable fortress was constructed by the Fitzalan family, lords of Clun and creators of the Norman borough here.

Protected on two sides by steep banks falling to the river, and on the others by the complex and massive earthworks of two ditched baileys, the strong-point of the castle is a rectangular stone keep. This, remarkably, was not built on top of the original motte, but to one side of it – as it were half on and half off –

perhaps in order to ensure a firm foundation: roughly constructed of slate rubble, it preserves several Norman windows. Apparently later still, the motte-top was ringed by a stone wall, of which two semi-circular thirteenth century towers remain.

On the other side of the River Clun, crossed in the middle of the town by a delightful medieval saddle-back bridge, is the parish church of St George, probably the centre of the settlement before the castle was built. The church contains a number of Norman features, but much the most striking is the squat, virtually windowless, and fortress-like tower. Topped by a wooden pyramid roof of later date, this tower was indeed almost certainly intended as a place of refuge, complementary to the nearby castle: and such defensive church towers are relatively common throughout this once-turbulent frontier region.

See **Castles of the Norman Conquest.**

CLUN Shropshire
OS 137 SO 298809
The small and attractive border town of Clun is twenty miles west of Ludlow, and stands on the A488, midway between Knighton and Bishop's Castle. To the west is the hill country of Clun Forest, and the impressive remains of Offa's Dyke, the eighth-century boundary between England and Wales.

The remarkable Norman keep of Clun Castle seen from the motte top, with the Welsh Border hills in the background. Above right, Clun church's sturdy fortress-tower stands sentinel over the graveyard.

The Battle of Hastings

In September 1066 King Harold Hardrada of Norway invaded England in alliance with King Harold of England's own brother, Tostig, the former Earl of Northumbria who had been banished in 1065. A Norwegian force landed at Riccall in Yorkshire and defeated the northern English earls Edwin and Morcar on the 20th of September at Gate Fulford, now a suburb of York.

As soon as he heard of the Norse invasion, Harold of England raised an army and marched nearly 200 miles northwards from London, which brought him to Tadcaster on the 24th of September. On the morning of Monday the 25th of September, according to the Anglo-Saxon Chronicle, he "went right on through York" to attack the unprepared Scandinavian army at Stamford Bridge, seven miles to the east of York. There is little reliable information about the ensuing battle, except that it was fought out on foot in the ancient Germanic and Viking fashion, resulting in an overwhelming victory for the English king. Harold Hardrada and Tostig were killed and the Norse army smashed. According to one account, only twenty of the original invasion fleet of 300 ships were required to carry the survivors home. Thus at Stamford Bridge Harold won one of the great battles of Anglo-Saxon history, and one which if it had not been for subsequent events would be far better known.

Just two days later, on the 27th of September, the Norman fleet sailed from Saint Valéry-sur-Somme on the evening tide, having at last obtained a favourable wind, after six weeks of waiting and praying. They landed at Pevensey unopposed, and there within the Roman and Saxon fort of *Anderida* built a castle. Subsequently they moved on to Hastings where they built another, which is shown in course of erection in the Bayeux Tapestry. About the 1st of October Harold received news of the Norman landing, reputedly during a celebratory feast being held at York. He immediately moved southwards once more to London, where he assembled a new army: and following a forced march of almost sixty miles arrived at the place which is now called Battle on the evening of Friday the 13th of October. According to the Anglo-Saxon Chronicle, he had the objective of taking William by surprise, "before all the army had come". Norman scouts, however, had warned William of Harold's approach, and before dawn on the morning of Saturday the 14th of October the Conqueror moved his forces to Pelham Hill, where the English could be observed. Harold drew up his soldiers on the ridge where the abbey and town of Battle now stand, while William deployed his forces on lower ground to the south. According to the chronicler William of Poitiers the battle began at 9.00 a.m., with the terrible sound of trumpets on both sides.

The armies seem to have been reasonably well matched, with between 5,000 and 7,000 men on each side. In the Norman camp, however, there was a substantial cavalry element; while the English army consisted entirely of infantry, their elite force being the Scandinavian housecarls armed with their notorious two-handed battle axes. The English adopted traditional tactics, including the very close formation known as the shield wall. The housecarls were concentrated in the centre around the king and his two brothers Gyrth and Leofwine. The whole army extended almost half a mile along the ridge.

William deployed the Norman army in three divisions: in the centre were the Normans under William himself, to the left the Bretons and to the right the "French". At the front of each division were the archers and crossbowmen, behind them were the heavy infantry, and at the rear there were the heavily armed and mounted knights. The attack was launched by the Normans in that order; and with the archers and infantry failing to make much headway the cavalry was soon in action. William of Poitiers observed that this "was a strange kind of battle, one side with all mobility and initiative and the other just resisting as though rooted to the soil".

Details of the battle which raged all day are difficult to disentangle from the various legends that have naturally arisen from this fateful conflict. At one stage, apparently, the Breton wing of the army began to weaken, the movement spread, and there was a rumour that Duke William had been killed. The loss of morale that followed was accompanied by an English advance down the hill. According to the story Norman spirit was only revived when William lifted his helmet to reveal his face. This scene is vividly depicted on the Bayeux Tapestry, where it is followed by a Norman counter-charge led by William himself, resulting in the destruction of those English who had broken ranks in pursuit.

The other principal story concerning the battle tells of the so-called "feigned flight", a technique which the Normans had previously used successfully elsewhere. The object was to lure the English soldiers from the ridge and then to turn and cut them down. The tactic appears to have been dramatically successful in this instance, but the English army still did not finally yield until the end of the day, when Harold himself was killed at the foot of his standard, his brothers having long since been slain. The remnants of the English army then broke ranks and were ruthlessly pursued and ridden down by the Normans. According to William of Poitiers:

"Now as the day declined the English army realised beyond doubt that they could no longer stand against the Normans. They knew that they were reduced by heavy losses; that the king himself, with his brothers and many magnates of the realm, had fallen; that those who still stood were almost drained of strength; that they could expect no help. They saw the Normans not much diminished by casualties, threatening them more keenly than at the beginning, as if they had found new strength in the fight; they saw that fury of the Duke who spared no one who resisted him; they saw that courage which could only find rest in victory. They therefore turned to flight . . ."

There followed the incident of the "Malfosse", where some of the pursued turned upon the pursuers and in the gathering gloom horses and armoured riders tumbled into a ravine. But after darkness had fallen William returned to the scene of his triumph, and the following day had Harold buried under an inscribed stone on the seashore near Hastings. William was later to found Battle Abbey, with the high altar of its church marking the very spot where Harold fell.

See **William the Conqueror.**

COLCHESTER CASTLE Essex
OS 168 TL 998252

Colchester is fifty miles north-east of London, via the A12(T). The castle, which now houses a museum, is near the town centre: and nearby are the impressive ruins of Norman St Botolph's Priory.

Built straddling the base of a Roman temple, the castle is of the most impressive surviving monuments of William the Conqueror's reign. The stone keep, the largest of Norman date in the country, was constructed under the supervision of Bishop Gundulf, who was also responsible for the White Tower in London; and the plans of the two keeps are closely comparable. Argument about the precise date of the beginning of the castle is likely to continue; but one possible explanation for building on such a grand scale is that the fortress was a response to the burning of the town by the Danes in 1071. A length of the ditch and ramparts which surrounded the keep and separated it from the outer bailey to the north are now incorporated into the park.

Battlements at first floor level, from the earliest phase of the keep, are visible on the east side. The second floor has more untidy coursing, and the third floor (which may never have been completed) does not survive. The Norman fabric includes re-used Roman bricks, some set in herringbone fash-ion, and Caen stone imported from France. At the south-east corner, the rounded apse of the chapel breaks the otherwise angular plan. In the earliest period the keep was probably entered by a stairway, and the present doorway, of decoratively carved Caen stone, was inserted in the late eleventh or twelfth century. Under the modern timber access bridge, the foundations of the early twelfth century outer defence works can be seen – a complicated arrangement involving a series of right-angled turns before reaching the keep door.

The interior of the castle has surviving Norman fireplaces, with herring-boned pattern-ing in the bricks at the back, and in the north-east corner is a fragment of the original floor of re-used Roman tiles. Crudely scratched drawings of Norman soldiers can be seen on the wall by the door. The great stairs to the south-west (with a turn of sixteen foot diameter) were reconstructed in the late eleventh or twelfth century, at the same time as the entrance.
See **Castles of the Norman Conquest.**

CORFE CASTLE Dorset
OS 195 SY 958823

Corfe Castle and village stand at the centre of the picturesque Isle of Purbeck, on the A351 midway between Swanage and Wareham.

The ruins of Corfe Castle keep, still impressive after centuries of battering by weather and warfare.

From whichever direction one approaches, the first view of Corfe castle is dramatic. Situated on top of an isolated chalk hill, it dominates the town and the whole Isle of Purbeck. Its history too has been dramatic. It was here that the Saxon king Edward the Martyr was killed in 978, and Henry I imprisoned his brother Robert here in 1106. During the Anarchy it was besieged by King Stephen's forces (in 1149) but held out for Matilda, defying all attempts to take it. It was a favourite with King John, who often stayed here, and incarcerated many nobles within, while Edward II was imprisoned here in 1326. Corfe was besieged again in the Civil War, finally falling to the Parliamentarians: thereafter it was slighted, and now stands in ruins.

What remains of the castle is still spectacular however, and there is much Norman work still visible, amid later buildings and alterations. The Old Hall, close to the north-west corner of the outer bailey wall, contains herring-bone masonry and was built in c.1080; and the wall that encloses the inner ward is also eleventh century. Within lies the most impressive Norman structure, the keep or King's Tower, the focus of the entire castle. Built in c.1105, parts of only three walls survive to any height. Entry was by way of a large staircase on the west side. Its height is no doubt emphasised by its position on the crown of the hill, but even in ruins it retains an air of solidity and massive strength: it is easy to see how it withstood the attacks of its numerous besiegers.

Situated in a deep wooded valley less than half a mile from the sea, Culbone possesses one of several churches claiming to be the smallest in England, its total length being only thirty-five feet. This is in fact slightly larger than the churches at Lullington (Sussex) and Upleatham (Cleveland), but these are incomplete and previously formed parts of larger churches.

Although the dedication to Saint Culbone or Beuno indicates a Celtic origin, the earliest surviving work is the two-light window in the north wall of the nave. This is thought to be Saxon, but must have been re-set when the present church was built in the late twelfth century, with the simple two-cell plan so characteristic of small Norman parish churches. Apart from its small size, the remarkable feature of Culbone is that the plan has remained scarcely altered. Inside there is little to be seen, apart from the late fourteenth century screen and the crude font, but this must always have been the case, and it is for rustic simplicity that the visitor comes to Culbone.

The walk to the church must be one of the loveliest to any place of worship in the British Isles. Although sometimes crowded in summer, the church will almost certainly be deserted in winter or early spring, with only the sound of the nearby stream for company.

CULBONE Somerset
OS 181 SS 842482
Culbone is eight miles west of Minehead, and is reached by turning north off the A39.

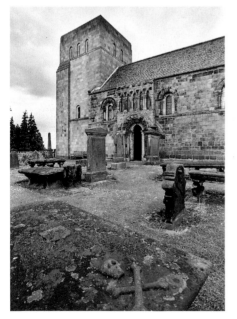

St Cuthbert's church at Dalmeny is perhaps the best preserved Romanesque parish church in Scotland. In plan there is a west tower, a nave with a north aisle giving into a narrower chancel, and then an apse. The whole church was built in a fine greyish-white limestone, probably at the instigation of Earl Gospatric in the mid-twelfth century.

As usual, the south door is a principal feature, projecting slightly forward from the wall-line with intersecting arcading above the arch. Deeply recessed, the arch is elaborately decorated, and especially striking are the finely carved heads spaced alternately with intricate interlaced motifs. There is no particular system to the subjects of the carvings – the signs of the Zodiac and the Lamb of God mingle in an erratic manner.

Before entering the church, the single-light round-headed windows are worthy of note for their sculptured capitals and arches. Once inside, the strikingly decorated arches of chancel and apse punctuate the interior

DALMENY Lothian
OS 65 NT 145775
Dalmeny is eight miles north-west of Edinburgh, just north of the A90 Forth Bridge road.

Emblems of mortality surround Dalmeny, Scotland's finest Norman parish church.

space. Supported on groups of three shafts, with scalloped capitals, the stones of the arches emphatically repeat the chevron decoration of the outer windows. Above both chancel and apse is some exceptionally fine vaulting: and the total effect, emphasised by the descending roof height, is to draw the eye rhythmically towards the central shaft of light shining on the altar through the central apse window.

It is well worth looking closely at the corbels supporting the vault ribs. They have been carved with both monster and human heads while, on the south side of the church, is a muzzled bear.

Despite appearances, the north aisle is mock-Romanesque work executed in 1671, with even later additions. The tower, although standing on the foundations of the original, was rebuilt in 1937.

The tunnel-like interior design of Dalmeny church draws the eye.

The castle dominates the town of Dover, which is seventy miles south-east of London via the A2 and M2. The Saxon church of St Mary-in-Castro, within the castle precincts, is well worth a visit, and in the town St Mary's church in Cannon Street has a sturdy Norman tower.

"The key of England". Dover Castle on its hilltop, with the tower of Saxon St. Mary-in-Castro to the left. Left, even after penetrating Dover's outermost defences, an attacker would still be faced with the inner curtain wall surrounding the keep.

After his victory at Hastings, the Conqueror marched along the south coast of England to Dover. There he set up camp within the great earthwork ramparts of an ancient Iron Age hill-top fort, which had subsequently been used as the site of a Roman lighthouse and of the Anglo-Saxon church of St Mary-in-Castro, both of which still survive. It is most likely, too, that in the years before the Con-

quest the prehistoric earthworks had defended a Saxon *burh* or fortified town: and it was here that William, according to his custom, raised a simple motte and bailey castle. This early Norman fortress continued in use until 1168, when Henry II began the construction of the present castle, one of the largest and probably the strongest of all medieval British fortifications.

Guarding the shortest Channel crossing to Europe, and hence aptly named 'the Key of England', this mighty stronghold is centred on a great four-square keep, some ninety-five feet high and roughly the same measurement in length and breadth, with walls up to twenty-one feet thick. Containing three main storeys of rooms, it can only be entered via an external forebuilding, so that an attacker had to fight his way through three towered gates and up three flights of stairs (originally open to the sky and the missiles of defenders) before he even reached the door of the keep proper. Neither was the spiritual welfare of the occupants neglected, for the keep includes two beautiful Norman chapels, one in the forebuilding and one on the second floor: while a well plunging deep into the chalk foundations below supplied the water vital to a besieged garrison.

As this complex and remarkably well-preserved keep was nearing completion, in about 1185, the king's masons set about surrounding it with a strongly fortified inner bailey wall. This is studded with no less than fourteen projecting rectangular towers, whose cross-fire swept every inch of the intervening wall: each tower, moreover, was a little fortress in itself, which could be used to seal off any section of the wall-top taken by the enemy; and the entire defensive line, being built lower than the keep, could additionally be covered by fire from the roof of that stronghold.

Not content even with this, Henry next began work on a second, outer, curtain wall, surrounding the inner bailey wall and in turn swept by its fire: this outer wall, eventually equipped with over thirty towers of its own, was to be completed by his son King John and grandson Henry III. But it was the second Henry's revolutionary master-plan which made Dover the earliest European castle known to have employed several concentric lines of defence, one within the other. His great fortress, moreover, remains substantially complete, and the traveller will do well to allot at least half a day to its detailed investigation.

See **Castles of the Norman Conquest.**

The Upper Chapel, one of two within Dover Castle's keep.

The abbey stands in a beautiful secluded setting on the north bank of the River Tweed, and is built of the attractive local pink sandstone. Founded in 1150, it was the first Scottish home of the canons regular of the Premonstratensian order. These "white canons" set out their abbey along similar lines to their parent house at Alnwick in Northumberland, with an aisled cruciform church 180 feet long, a cloister eighty-five feet square, and an eastern and southern range. A high wall enclosed the cloister instead of the usual west range. As at Jedburgh, the monastic buildings were terraced into the river bank, with the abbey church overlooking the cloisters and the river. The abbey was a victim of several border campaigns between the English and the Scots, being seriously damaged on a number of occasions.

both, however, thought to have been carved in the thirteenth century – probably while stonemasons were working in the abbey.

Apart from some later alterations, the monastic buildings are Norman and thirteenth century: in the east range there is a vestry, parlour, chapter house, daystair, warming house, passage and novices' room, with the canons' and novices' dormitories on the first floor. The east door from the church into the cloisters and the doorway into the chapter house are richly decorated, and although the warming house fireplace was removed, that in the novices' day room is original. In the southern range are the remains of the subcroft where provisions were stored, before being prepared in the kitchen (now demolished) and eaten in the refectory above. A channel was cut to bring fresh water from the

DRYBURGH ABBEY Borders
OS 74 NT 591317
The abbey stands one mile north of St Boswells and four miles south-east of Melrose, and is reached via a minor road turning east off the A68. Dryburgh is thus conveniently situated midway between two other notable border abbeys, those at Melrose and Jedburgh: and in countryside remarkable both for its natural beauty and its profusion of historic buildings.

Through this doorway in the cloister Dyrburgh's "white canons" entered their chapter house, which preserves rare fragments of Norman wall paintings.

This abbey is unusual in that most of the earliest surviving building phases belong to the claustral and domestic ranges rather than the church. It therefore provides a rare opportunity to see predominantly Norman monastic buildings. It is also very special because fragments of twelfth century decorative painting survive in the chapter house.

The original abbey church was dedicated to St Mary, but very little remains today. The west end was reconstructed in the fifteenth century. It is worth noting the scratches on a foundation stone in the ruined north wall of the nave: they represent a board for the game of *merelles* (which was introduced into England by the Normans) and there are only two known examples of such boards in Scotland – here and at Arbroath Abbey. They are

Tweed.

The chapter house has a barrel vault with stone benches around the walls, and it is here that traces of twelfth century decoration survive: on the east wall the spaces between the stone blind arcading have been decorated with painted geometric and semi-naturalistic leaf patterns. The design of the blind arcading has also been carried round the other walls with a painted surface rather than stone carvings. The colours are red, black and white. In addition fragments of mural paintings survive on the vaulting of the north window. Although these traces serve as a sad reminder of all the medieval surface decoration that has been lost throughout Britain, their very rarity make them particularly valuable here.
See **Jedburgh Abbey.**

William the Conqueror

The boy who was to become William the Conqueror, greatest alike of the dukes of Normandy and of the Norman kings of England, was born at Falaise in 1027 or 1028. At the time of his birth, nevertheless, there was little to indicate that he would become either a duke or a king: and his only title – by which, indeed, he was to be known for most of his life – was William the Bastard. For he was the illegitimate son of Duke Robert I of Normandy and a local girl called Herleve or Arlette, the daughter of a Falaise tanner: a descent of which his enemies were prone to remind him, on one occasion by hanging untanned hides from the walls of a town he was besieging. In 1035, however, his father died suddenly, while still unmarried and in his twenties: and the seven year old William, his only heir, became Duke of Normandy. His accession was anything but smooth, and his minority was spent in a court which was notoriously anarchic and bloodstained even by the standards of the time – three of his guardians, indeed, were in turn assassinated, one in the boy's own bedchamber: and though he defeated a dangerous revolt at the battle of Val-ès-Dunes in 1047, many years of more or less continuous warfare followed before William finally made himself master of the Duchy. Not until about 1060, then, could he safely turn his mind to his claim on the English throne.

This claim derived not from hereditary right, but from William's nomination as heir by the then King of England, the childless Edward the Confessor. The son of Aethelred the Unready by William's great-aunt (the formidable Emma, sister of Duke Richard II of Normandy) Edward was half Norman by birth: and having spent his early life in exile in the Duchy, the English king was more than half Norman in his cultural and political preferences. But his choice of William as his successor (apparently confirmed in 1051) infuriated the greatest and most unscrupulous of his English subjects, the family of Earl Godwin: and though in 1064 Harold Godwinson, by then the most powerful man in England, was induced under somewhat suspicious circumstances to swear an oath supporting William's claim, Harold himself seized the throne when Edward died on the 5th of January 1066.

On hearing this news, the indignant Duke at once began raising an invasion force and building a fleet to carry it across the Channel. This fleet finally sailed on September the 27th, and in the Hastings campaign that followed William decisively defeated Harold and gained control of southern England, being crowned King of England at Westminster Abbey on Christmas Day 1066. But five more years of intermittent fighting – including the savage campaign of devastation called "the Harrying of the North" – were necessary before the king was in full control of his new realm, and even then he had to be continually on his guard against fresh revolts and Scandinavian invasions. Despite these difficulties in England, moreover, William had to spend more than half his twenty-one year reign dealing with the equally pressing problems of Normandy. It was there, during a typically brutal sack of the town of Mantes, that the king fell mortally ill – as a result, according to one report, of rupturing himself on the saddle-pommel of his rearing horse: and on the 9th of September 1087 the great Conqueror died at Rouen.

It is scarcely surprising that this remarkable man made a deep impression on his contemporaries, several of whom have left descriptions of him. He was, it seems, "great in body and strong", and his remains indicate that he stood some five feet ten inches in height, considerably taller than most men of his day: he must, therefore, have towered above his diminutive wife Matilda, who was only four foot two – but who had ten children by him, including his successors William Rufus and Henry I. He was also described as "majestic" and "not ungainly", but he apparently grew very fat in his later years, despite his unusual abstemiousness in eating and drinking: indeed, his atttendants had considerable difficulty in forcing his swollen body into its stone coffin. His voice was noticeably harsh, doubtless from much shouting on battlefields, but his speech was fluent and persuasive, and "what he said was always well suited to the occasion".

Both his Norman and his English subjects also praised his personal piety and great wisdom: but one of the latter, who had lived at his court, dwells too upon the darker aspects of his character. King William, he admits, was kind enough to monks and holy men, and his stern justice kept such good order in England that a man might ride unmolested through it from one end to the other, though his bosom were full of gold. Yet he was "cruel beyond measure to those who opposed his will", dispossessing and imprisoning without mercy anyone who resisted him, earl, bishop or abbot. Nor did he spare the common folk.

> "A hard man was the king
> He took from his subjects many marks of gold
> And hundreds of pounds in silver
> Most unjustly and for little cause
> For he was sunk in greed
> And altogether given to avarice . . .
> The rich complained of it, the poor lamented it
> But so relentless was he that he cared nothing for their hate
> And all were compelled, if they wished to keep life and lands
> To submit themselves entirely to his will"

The facts of his life, too, show that the Conqueror was a terrible, harsh and ruthless man, as well as a pious, clever, energetic and extraordinarily resourceful one: but he lived in harsh and terrible times, and his upbringing can scarcely have predisposed him to gentleness. It may well be, indeed, that only a ruler with William's particular combination of qualities could have dominated and controlled first Normandy and then England.
See **The Battle of Hastings.**

DUNFERMLINE ABBEY Fife
OS 65 NT 097875

Dunfermline stands near the north end of the Forth Road Bridge, and is reached from Edinburgh via the A90 and the M90, turning off the latter at junction 2. The abbey is in the town centre, off Canmore Street.

Christ Church, Dunfermline is one of the earliest abbeys in Scotland, having been founded as a Benedictine house by Queen Margaret in about 1072: it was a daughter-institution of the cathedral priory of Christ Church at Canterbury. Excavations have shown that it was built over a small pre-Conquest church which comprised a rectangular single-cell building with a square western tower. At some time in the tenth or eleventh century, a square choir with a rounded apse was added on the east side. This characteristically Romanesque apse represents the introduction of the style to Scotland and the plan of this early church, of great historic importance, is shown on the nave paving of the succeeding church, which was begun in 1128.

The twelfth century re-building by King David I survives principally in the marvellous

nave, considered to be the finest Romanesque interior in Scotland. Especially interesting is the bold incised decoration of the pillars of the arcade and the very simple ornamentation of the arches. The manner and style of this decorative treatment has led to a suggestion of links with Durham Cathedral, which was nearing completion when the twelfth century rebuilding began at Dunfermline. Perhaps this may be explained partly by a natural desire to have the latest and proudest architectural fashion, and partly by the recruitment of skilled masons from the Durham workforce.

Besides being an important abbey, Christ Church was also a royal mausoleum. Margaret, the founder, was the first of many Scottish kings and queens to be buried here. The ruins of the later royal palace can be seen nearby in a public park.

DURHAM
OS 88 NZ 273420

Durham, fourteen miles south of Newcastle and seventy miles north of York, is easily reached from the A1 trunk road.

The city is still physically dominated by the castle and cathedral on the rock of the peninsula, and there are spectacular views of this relationship from the various bridges over the Wear, from the surrounding hills and also from the railway station.

The present layout of the city on the peninsula also continues to reflect the early medieval street pattern, which was determined by the Norman settlement. The market place lies to the north of, and very clearly outside, the castle-cathedral precinct, with the main east-west axis lying between the two twelfth century bridges of Framwellgate and Elvet (both largely rebuilt). The main street runs the length of the peninsula, along the line of the old north and south baileys of the castle, while the narrow alleys or vennels run between properties. Intriguingly hidden behind the predominantly Georgian facade of many of the town houses, the structure of much earlier buildings often survives relatively intact.

The castle was first built on the orders of William I, on his return from Scotland in 1072, and placed under the control of the Bishops of Durham. Together with that at Newcastle, this castle was the only tangible sign of early Norman feudal authority north of the River Tees.

It is located on the neck of the peninsula, at its most vulnerable and yet most easily defensible spot, guarding the river crossing. It had inner and outer moats and baileys, and the cathedral and monastery were well protected within the bailey walls. It was only much later, in the fourteenth century, that the market place and the burghers were also protected by a wall to the north of the castle defences.

The Norman chapel is thought to be part of this early castle (*c.*1080) and is the oldest part of the building to survive intact. The capitals are decorated with barbaric faces and beasts, which contrast dramatically with the

somewhat later and more formal Norman non-figurative decoration to be seen in other parts of the castle, and in the cathedral. The Norman work which still survives at the castle includes the gatehouse, the undercroft chapel, and the gallery in the north range.

William I gave the Bishops of Durham vice-regal powers in order to control the North of England, and if necessary to fight the Scots. To this end, the Bishop was empowered to maintain his own army and have his own exchequer, mint, and law courts. Durham city was his administrative centre and the castle was therefore not only used as a military stronghold but also became the Bishop's main palace. It was occupied as such until the early nineteenth century, when Bishop Van Mildert gave it to the new university.

A Benedictine monastery was founded in Durham in *c.*1071 and the cathedral, intended as a monastic cathedral, was begun in 1092, replacing an existing church which housed the bones and relics of the Saxon saint Cuthbert, brought to Durham in 995. Although the monastery was dissolved in 1539, several of its buildings and the precinct survive, to the south of the cathedral – including the cloisters and the monks' dormitory (fourteenth century).

The cathedral, built of local sandstone, took forty years to complete. The beautiful Galilee Chapel was added to the west end in the late twelfth century, and we are lucky that fragments of its contemporary frescoes have survived restoration. The lightness of the arcading and the slenderness of the pillars may perhaps reflect a Moorish influence on Norman architecture, percolating through from Norman contacts in Sicily and North Africa.

The west towers were completed in the early thirteenth century, and apart from the heightening of the tower in the fifteenth century, the last major change was the replacement of the original apsidal east end by the

Chapel of the Nine Altars in the second half of the fourteenth century.

The most important early source of information about the cathedral is the Chronicle of Symeon of Durham, written in about *c*.1105. From this it is known that the design and early building phases may be attributed to Bishop William of St Calais, who came over with William the Conqueror. He subsequently spent three years in exile in Normandy during the 1080s, and the design of Durham Cathedral doubtless owes much to the great abbeys he would have seen being built there.

Durham Cathedral is the most intact example of prestigious Norman ecclesiastical architecture that survives in Britain, and is justifiably famous for its structurally and stylistically innovative features. Durham has the earliest stone ribbed and vaulted roof in Northern Europe. The choir was rib-vaulted in *c*.1104, this being thirty years earlier than the rib-vaults in the first great "Gothic" cathedral, at St Denis in France. Unfortunately the choir roof cracked badly and had to be rebuilt in the mid thirteenth century, but the original cross-rib vault of the aisles may still be seen today. The transverse arches supporting the nave are probably the earliest pointed arches in England, and the interlaced wall arcading and the deeply grooved spiral, lozenge and chevron designs on the pillars are also the first of their kind in Britain, although these ideas were soon to be repeated at Holy Island, Norwich, Waltham, Selby and the crypt at York Minster.

Although visitors today are impressed by the undeniable grandeur, simplicity, and strength of the architecture (characterised by the massive pillars whose girth equals their height!), it is important to remember that before the Reformation our impression of the interior would have been completely different. For, as in all churches, the bare stonework would originally have been plastered,

Top left, the gracefully slender pillars of Durham Cathedral's Galilee Chapel suggest a Moorish influence on Norman architecture. Top right, incised decoration on a mighty pillar, one of the hallmarks of Durham's Norman masons. Above, looking through a Norman arch into the courtyard of Durham Castle.

and the surface heavily decorated with geometric designs. The predominant colours in Durham were red, black and white, and there are still traces clearly visible in the south aisle.

EAST MEON

OS 185 SU 681223

All Saints church lies at the foot of a steep hill in the pretty village of East Meon, which is four miles west of Petersfield via the A272 and a minor road. East of the church is a Court House of c.1400, which once belonged to the Bishops of Winchester.

A distinctive spire caps East Meon's Norman tower. Opposite, this fine black Tournai marble font was probably given to the church by Henry of Blois, a famous Bishop of Winchester.

This impressive church is built on a cruciform plan, and the tower is a powerful expression of Norman architecture. Externally the decoration suggests a mid twelfth century date; while internally the arches of the crossing suggest an early twelfth century date! Internally the crossing and the transepts are the most interesting features. The east and west arches are nicely decorated with scalloped capitals, while the north and south arches are plain.

The west and south doorways also provide fine examples of mid twelfth century work. The west doorway is the most elaborate with its fluted leaf capitals. The south doorway was reset in the wall of the south aisle of the nave during the construction of the aisle during the late thirteenth century. The church also contains a splendid example of a black Tournai marble font of about 1140, with figure sculpture of Adam and Eve scenes.

EDINBURGH CASTLE
OS 66 NT 251735

The castle, one of the most visited monuments in Britain, is open all the year round: and the fine city of Edinburgh contains a wealth of places of interest.

Spectacularly situated on a rocky outcrop, with splendid views over the city, the masonry of Edinburgh castle rises as if it were a natural extension of the rock face. Massive curtain walls encompassing the bailey, and the citadel grouped around Palace Yard, follow the contours of the rock. The whole effect emphasises the power and prestige of the principal Scottish royal castle.

Edinburgh rock has been a fortress from time immemorial, but the recorded history of the castle begins during the eleventh century reign of King Malcolm Canmore, when it was probably defended by a stockade. Within this line of defence, the first set of stone buildings was erected, and of these the principal surviving structure is St Margaret's Chapel, whose dedication is linked directly to the holy life of Malcolm's queen.

Of the Norman work in the chapel, the most unusual feature is the remarkable plan. The building externally is square ended, but on entering, a glance down the nave shows a semi-circular stone vaulted apse. A considerable amount of restoration has taken place, but the chancel arch with its sculptured decoration is original: and so too is the westernmost of the three small round-headed windows on the south side of the nave. Outside, the check for holding the Norman wooden window frame can be seen. Externally, the lower parts of the walls are of fine red and grey ashlar blocks. The upper part has been reconstructed, but the evidence of charters shows the chapel to have been complete by 1130.

Depicted in modern stained glass, the saintly Queen Margaret gazes into her chapel in Edinburgh Castle.

ELY CATHEDRAL
Cambridgeshire
OS 143 TL 541802

Ely is fifteen miles north of Cambridge, on the A10(T): the cathedral, which stands in the middle of the small city, is visible for many miles around in this flat Fenland country.

Considerable sections of the Norman church survive, namely part of the lavishly decorated west front exterior, with its central tower: and, within, the lengthy nave and transepts. These interior features, though very finely proportioned, are largely without ornament, contrasting with the richly carved Norman 'prior's door' and 'monks' door', both leading from the cloister into the church. Such Norman remains tend to be overshadowed by those parts of the cathedral magnificently reconstructed in the fourteenth century, and in particular by the wonderful 'octagon' built to replace the collapsed Norman central tower: but nonetheless they are well worth seeking out by the traveller in search of Norman England.

The great Fenland monastery of Ely was originally founded in 673 by the Saxon princess St Etheldreda, but subsequently it was destroyed by the Vikings and re-founded as a Benedictine abbey in 970. Soon after the Norman Conquest it became the centre of the Anglo-Saxon resistance led by the hero Hereward the Wake, suffering further damage: then, in 1081, a relative of King William's named Simeon was appointed abbot, and though he was already eighty-six years old, he was to live another dozen years and begin the construction of a great new Norman abbey church. Building continued throughout the twelfth century, being completed in about 1189: and meanwhile, in 1109, Ely became the cathedral of a new diocese created from part of the enormous Saxon see of Lincoln.

Left, beautifully carved "Priors Door" at Ely, leading from the cloister into the cathedral, is surmounted by a figure of Christ in Majesty. Above, the plain but immensely impressive Norman nave at Ely, looking eastwards towards the central octagon.

Ewenny, a name meaning 'bright water', was a Benedictine house founded in the early twelfth century. It is remarkable for the substantial survival of its original fortified precinct wall, complete with towers, and for the massive central tower of the church, both suggesting the importance of defence. The site is one of great beauty, overlooking the river from which it took its name and the broad meadows stretching towards Bridgend. To the south-west is Ogmore and the sea. Ewenny is a characteristically Norman foundation, in the rich agricultural coastal plain, linked to a chain of castles including Bridgend and Ogmore: yet the extensive and important finds of Celtic sculpture here point to the existence of a previous Welsh monastery. On this evidence it is probable that the foundation by Maurice de Londres was part of a deliberate policy of Normanisation. The close link with the monastery at Gloucester after 1141 suggests that Norman monks came from there with the intention of displacing the hostile Celtic community.

The main Norman work can be seen in the nave, choir and transept. Overall, the impression is of simplicity and ruggedness. The piers of the north aisle are massive, yet with only minimal scallop carving on the capitals: while the windows of both nave and choir are deep, narrow, round-headed, and almost devoid of ornamentation. This work has been dated to no later than 1120. The former west door, now set in the gardens of the priory, also has only very plain chevron moulding, consistent with a date perhaps even as early as the late eleventh century.

Soon after the church was built, a screen was constructed to divide it in two. The nave was used as the parochial church, the remainder by the monks: an economical and effective arrangement. As usual, the cloister lay on the south side. Much was demolished in the nineteenth century, but the prior's lodging survives in the western range.

One of the most interesting features of the priory church is the complete founder's tomb-slab. It is bordered by finely carved scroll work, and a graceful foliated cross divides the simple two-line inscription: 'Here lies Maurice de Londres, the Founder, God reward him for his work. Amen'.

EWENNY Mid Glamorgan
OS 170 SS 913778
The priory is just over a mile south of Bridgend, on the B4524: it may also be reached from Swansea or Cardiff via junction 35 of the M4 motorway and the A48(T).

FOUNTAINS ABBEY

North Yorkshire
OS 99 SE 274683

The abbey is four miles south-west of Ripon, whence it is well signposted via the B6265 and a minor road. An interesting site museum contains a useful model of the monastery as it appeared in its heyday: and the River Skell, flowing by the ruins, is notable for its wild flowers and birds. Fountains Hall, built with abbey stone, is seventeenth century.

The splendid and extensive ruins of Fountains Abbey, landscaped in the eighteenth century, are of European significance, both for the completeness of their Cistercian ground-plan and for the material evidence of the development of Cistercian monasticism in the late Middle Ages.

The house was founded in 1132 by a small group of monks from the wealthy Benedictine abbey of St Mary's, York, who sought greater austerity and purity in their religious life. They were encouraged and helped by Archbishop Thurstan of York (1114–40) who settled them on his estates in the then wild and inhospitable country of Skeldale.

Monks who left their monastery and abandoned their order were not popular; and although the monks were formally received as Cistercians in 1133, and despite links with Rievaulx and even with the great Saint Bernard of Clairvaux himself (1090–1153), the early years of the community were difficult, due to a lack of lay confidence and financial support. Until 1135 the future of the community was in doubt, but in that year it received endowments from a number of wealthy clergy from York Minister, who chose to end their days as monks in the new community. Once the abbey was on a secure economic footing and was clearly going to survive, it attracted much economic support from all sections of society. So much so that the monks could mount almost continuous building programmes from 1138 to 1250, with substantial additions being made right up to the eve of the Dissolution in 1539.

The whole south wall of the nave, together with the eastern half of the north wall and the whole of the cloister, belong to the primary building of 1138–50. To the 1150s may be assigned the remainder of the north wall of the nave and the fine Galilee porch at the west end of the church – a particular feature of early Cistercian houses – while the chapter house and all the buildings on the east side of the cloister date from the 1160s–80s. The remainder of the magnificent ruins belong to a later date, but their arrangement provides an excellent insight into the life of a medieval monastic community.

Fountains has a beautiful setting with fine trees, a river, a lake and footpaths through both formal gardens and wooded terraces. It well repays an extended visit.
See **Rievaulx Abbey.**

Above, although dominated by a great sixteenth-century tower, the extensive and well-preserved ruins of Fountains Abbey are mainly of late Norman date. Right, the entrance to the large and stately chapter house, whose size testifies to the success of this wealthy Yorkshire community.

The abbey was originally founded by Stephen of Blois near Preston, for monks of the Savignac order. In 1127 the monks moved to this more remote site and were richly endowed by Stephen after he became king in 1135. The abbey became extremely prosperous with large agricultural and iron-mining interests, as well as owning property in Ireland and the Isle of Man. In 1147 Stephen unsuccessfully resisted its amalgamation with the Cistercian order, and at the time of the Dissolution in 1535 it was England's second richest Cistercian abbey after Fountains Abbey.

Today the beautiful red sandstone ruins of the abbey are particularly dramatic: they are set in "The Vale of Deadly Nightshade", a sheltered natural bowl adjacent to a stream

FURNESS ABBEY Cumbria
OS 96 SD 218717
Furness Abbey is one and a half miles north-north-east of Barrow-in-Furness, off the A590. Barrow can be reached from junction 36 of the M6 motorway (forty miles away to the east) via the A6 and A590 westwards, a picturesque route which skirts the Lake District and the Cumbrian coast.

and surrounded by wooded slopes with sheep pastures. The ruins of the precinct wall of the monastery follow the rim of the bowl, enhancing the secluded nature of the site. The narrow terrain has demanded an unusual layout for the abbey, and its size is impressive: the 200 foot long dormitory, 126 foot infirmary and 150 foot refectory are comparable with their equivalents at Fountains Abbey.

The present ruins are principally of the later Cistercian house, which was begun in

the mid twelfth century. Although little remains above the foundations in the south and west parts of the site, the choir, transepts and east cloister range still stand to roof level, providing fine examples of late Norman architecture. The ornate arches of the chapter house and adjoining entrances illustrate the Savignac taste for fine decoration, which was initially disapproved of by the Cistercians. This richness can also be seen at Byland in North Yorkshire, which was colonised from Furness.

Time has weathered the red sandstone arches of Furness Abbey, but the choir and transepts of the abbey church still stand to their original full height.

51

Above, these round arches leading into Furness Abbey's chapter house contrast with the slightly later pointed arch leading out of it.

Gloucester was important to William the Conqueror both because of its traditional connections with the English royal house and because of its command of a strategic crossing of the Severn. In 1072, therefore, he determined to revive the long-established but moribund Saxon monastery here, appointing his own chaplain Serlo as its abbot. Serlo set about building a great Norman abbey church in 1089, and by the time of his death in 1104 (the number of monks having meanwhile increased from two to a hundred) the crypt and the choir above it were finished. His successors continued the work, so that by about 1160 the Norman nave had been constructed, and the body of the present church – which became a cathedral in 1541 – was complete.

The Norman nave survives substantially unaltered, as does Serlo's early Norman crypt, with its squat pillars and massive arches designed to bear the weight of the choir overhead, which almost exactly follows its plan. This choir, however, was greatly altered in the fourteenth century, when the revenue derived from pilgrims flocking to the tomb-shrine of the murdered King Edward II allowed the monks to sumptuously reconstruct their church in the latest Perpendicular style. Using the Norman choir pillars as supports (they are still visible, as it were behind the scenes) the masons built soaring stone screens, topped by a magnificent roof and framing the famous great east window which replaced the Norman apse. The aisles of the east end, nevertheless, remain as the Normans built them.

Most of the surviving monastic buildings at Gloucester, including the splendid fanvaulted cloister, were also reconstructed in the fourteenth century. But the chapter house retains much Norman work, and it was here, at Christmas 1085, that King William and his barons planned the making of Domesday Book. The Conqueror's eldest son, Robert Duke of Normandy, was also a patron of Gloucester Abbey: and here, having fallen foul of his younger brother Henry I and died in captivity, he lies buried under a brightly painted thirteenth-century tomb. *See* **The Domesday Book.**

GLOUCESTER CATHEDRAL
Gloucestershire
OS 162 SO 831188

Gloucester is 109 miles north-west of London, via the M40 and A40. Visitors to the cathedral (which is clearly visible, dominating the city) should also see the tomb of the murdered King Edward II, and the splendid fourteenth century monastic cloister. In the city, the medieval churches of St Mary de Crypt (Southgate Street) and St Nicholas (Westgate Street) are of interest.

Goodrich Castle stands on a high spur of land on the west bank of the River Wye, commanding an ancient crossing of the river. "Godric's castle" is first mentioned about 1101. No remains of this early castle can now be identified, but it is possible that the rock-cut moat follows the line of its defences. The earliest surviving work is the square keep on the south side of the enclosure, which was probably built by the middle of the twelfth century. This fine keep is of three stages: the original doorway, a plain arched opening now converted into a window, is on the first floor, and was reached by an external staircase. The shafts on either side of it have scalloped capitals and moulded bases. The Norman windows also survive in the upper storey. The keep is hemmed in by later and more massive fortifications marking the ebb and flow of Welsh Marcher warfare, but its graceful lines still mark it out as something special.

GOODRICH CASTLE
Herefordshire
OS 162 SO 577200

The castle is four miles south-west of Ross-on-Wye, via the A40(T) and a signposted minor road: the views from it are superb, and nearby the Wye cuts through the spectacularly wooded Symond's Yat gorge.

HARDHAM CHURCH
West Sussex
OS 197 TQ 038176

The church stands just off the A29, one mile south of Pulborough and twenty miles north-east of Chichester: not far to the south are Parham House and medieval Amberley Castle.

Twelfth-century wall paintings adorn the walls of Hardham church.

The eleventh century church of St Botolph is now peacefully set back from the busy main road, on a loop of the old road which has been abandoned in favour of a more direct route. The church, built mainly of local sandstone and ironstone rubble, with some Roman bricks in the chancel, has large blocks of sandstone for its corners. It has preserved its original form almost unchanged, except for the addition of a porch to protect the north door. The church still consists of the original aisleless square-ended chancel and rectangular nave. There is a small bell-cote on the eastern end of the nave.

The church is chiefly known for its outstanding series of twelfth century wall paintings around the chancel and nave. They were first discovered in 1866 and are thought to be the earliest in the country. The scenes depict Adam and Eve, episodes in the life of Christ, the Apostles, the story of St George, and Heaven and Hell. Such paintings must originally have adorned the walls of many, if not all, early medieval churches, and played an important part in illustrating the preaching of the Gospels.

HEATH CHAPEL Shropshire
OS 137 SO 557857

The remote chapel is some seven miles north-east of Ludlow, and about a mile north of Clee St Margaret. It is best reached by taking the B4365/ B4368 road from Ludlow towards Much Wenlock, and turning east at Diddlebury onto a minor road to Tugford. After about two miles turn south through Peaton and Bouldon towards Abdon, and the chapel is just north of the road, shortly before the hamlet of Upper Heath.

This almost perfect example of a Norman chapel stands high up in the foothills of the Brown Clee Hill in southern Shropshire. It was originally a dependent chapel of its mother church at Stoke St Milborough, which in turn was almost certainly founded from Wenlock Priory in the mid-Saxon period.

The chapel consists of a single cell nave and chancel, with no post-Norman alterations to the plan. The fabric of the church is primarily Norman, although a new roof replaced the ancient wooden shingles at the beginning of this century. The south doorway is Norman with a plain tympanum, but the local sandstone used for building has been heavily eroded. On the inside is a plain Norman circular font and medieval wall paintings: these are in poor condition, but one clearly depicts St George slaying the dragon. The ancient box pews, dating from the seventeenth century, are a distinctive feature of the cool dark interior of this splendid edifice. The chapel stands at the centre of an extensive area of earthworks, representing the village which once occupied the site.
See **Much Wenlock Priory.**

HEREFORD CATHEDRAL
Herefordshire
OS 149 SO 510398

Hereford is 145 miles north-west of London, via the M40, A40, M5, M50 and A438. Apart from the cathedral and its chained library, the visitor should also see the medieval city walls, and explore the maze of ancient narrow streets to the north of the cathedral close.

Hereford is one of Britain's less-visited cathedrals, which is a pity because, although rather heavily restored in the late eighteenth and nineteenth centuries, it contains some of the most splendid Norman architecture in the country.

The diocese is one of the oldest in England and dates back to about 676: but, unlike many other cathedrals, Hereford was never monastic. The present building is mainly the work of two of the first Norman bishops, Robert de Losinga (1079–1095) and Reynelm (1107–1115). The nave was completed under Bishop Robert of Bethune, who was buried in the cathedral in 1148.

Of this first Norman church, the nave, chancel, and parts of the crossing and south transept are the principal survivals. The earliest work is in the east wall of the south transept, with its five tiers of round arches dating from the late eleventh or the early twelfth century. The contemporary fireplace on the opposite wall is an unusual feature, the only other known example being that in a similar position at Durham Cathedral.

The chancel is a little later and probably dates from around 1120. The main arcade and the gallery above are unmistakably Norman, the pointed-arched clerestory and vault being Early English work of about 1240. The eastern arch, now opening into the retrochoir, is mid nineteenth century, but some of the original capitals have been preserved and are displayed in the corridor to the Vicars' College. They are primitively carved and are said to be in the Anglo-Saxon tradition. To the left and right of the main east arch (the arcading above incidentally is Victorian) are the eastern arches of the choir aisles, which originally terminated in semi-circular Norman chapels. Above them, on the east side, are blocked windows.

Little remains of Norman work in the north transept, which was brilliantly reconstructed by Bishop Aquablanca in the mid thirteenth century, but the crossing arches are largely original, although the pillars beneath were entirely re-built as part of an underpinning operation in the mid nineteenth century. The present tower is early fourteenth century.

The best Norman work at Hereford is probably in the nave. The massive circular piers have twin shafts designed to carry the tie beams of an original wooden roof, and there is conspicuous chevron ornament on the arches. Everything above the main arcade, however, is the work of Wyatt, the late eighteenth century restorer. Also in the nave is the sadly mutilated font of about 1140, with unusual Greek-key ornament around the rim and an arcade of twelve arches with figures of the apostles below: it is supported by curious Norman lions and is the work of the renowned Hereford School of masons, whose fonts are also to be seen in a number of parish churches in the neighbourhood.

Before leaving the cathedral, the visitor should seek out the unique late twelfth century wooden chair in the chancel, said to be the one on which King Stephen was crowned; the famous 'Mappa Mundi' – a map of the world as it was known in the thirteenth century; and the chained-book library in a chamber above the north transept.

Between these two massive pillars stands Hereford Cathedral's fine Norman font, guarded by lions. Below, five tiers of variously decorated arches in the south transept are the earliest surviving Norman work at Hereford.

The Hereford School of Architecture

In the 150 years following the Norman Conquest there was a frenzy of church building throughout England and Wales. In some cases standing Anglo-Saxon structures were rebuilt, but a substantial number of entirely new parish churches were also erected. All these buildings were constructed in the style which we know as Norman. Norman architecture in Britain however was not identical throughout the country. There were clear regional distinctions, which developed particularly from the early decades of the twelfth century onwards, and there appear to have been schools of architecture (such as those based on Canterbury and Yorkshire) which used particular regional decorative designs.

Another of these schools was that which operated in the Welsh Marches and is known as the Herefordshire School, which like other schools appears to have relied heavily on the use of pattern books. The Herefordshire School came into being during the mid twelfth century, paradoxically at the height of a civil war. Shobdon church in northern Herefordshire was erected at this time and it appears that in this building the style of sculpture of the Herefordshire School began. There is a remarkable document preserved in the University Library at Chicago which tells of the foundation of the church. It was the work of Oliver de Merlimond, who was chief steward to Hugh de Mortimer, Lord of Wigmore. We hear that Oliver went on a pilgrimage to Santiago de Compostela in north-western Spain, following the pilgrimage route of St. James. It appears that he was heavily influenced by the pilgrimage architecture he encountered along the route, particularly on the Poitou region of western France and in the Burgos area of northern Spain.

Shobdon was regrettably pulled down in the eighteenth century, but its two doorways with their once-magnificent tympana and its chancel arch were re-erected in Shobdon Park as a triumphal arch, and over the years these have sadly suffered badly from weathering. The style of the sculpture incorporates a wide range of styles and motifs, some being Anglo-Saxon while others are Scandinavian, and still others seem to have come directly from churches along the pilgrimage route. Today the best surviving church of the Herefordshire School is at Kilpeck, just to the south-west of Hereford, which still has a wealth of twelfth century sculpture lavished on its doorway, chancel arch, corbel and windows. The main arch is carved with beak heads, monsters and an angel placed at the apex, while the label (moulding over the arch) has a chain motif, each ring containing a bird or monster and one the Fishes of the Zodiac. The doorway jambs are covered with the bodies of twisting snakes and one of the shafts with figures of warriors intertwining with foliage, while the other is carved with foliage and a pair of doves at the base. The capitals are decorated with animals and a grotesque head. On the tympanum a vine scroll forms a symmetrical design. The only conventional Anglo-Norman motifs used in the decoration of this doorway are the star pattern on the abaci (slabs over the capitals) and the chevron on the arch and lintel. The beak heads show a great variety of design.

The exterior of the church includes a richly decorated west window and a fine set of corbels carved in the form of grotesque heads and animals. These include a *sheila-na-gig*, or fertility symbol. Projecting from the angles of the nave on the west front are large heads of dragons carved in a style reminiscent of Scandinavian art.

The decoration of the chancel arch at Kilpeck consists of Anglo-Norman geometrical enrichment on the arch, but the shafts have a motif which until then was completely unknown in England. Each shaft is decorated with figures of three apostles one above the other. The source for this design appears to have come directly from the Puerta de las Platerias at Santiago de Compostela.

Other churches in the region used designs which could only have come from western France or northern Spain, such as the tympana at Brinsop and Stretton Sugwas, both in Herefordshire. In addition to these churches the Herefordshire School is represented by elaborate Romanesque decoration at Leominster Priory and Ralston church, tympana at Fownhope, Hereford and Ruardean (Gloucs) and fonts at Stottesdon (Salop) and Orleton. Sections of work carried out by members of the Herefordshire School or heavily influenced by them can also be seen at a considerable number of other churches, particularly in southern Shropshire.

IFFLEY CHURCH Oxfordshire
OS 164 SP 527035

The church is roughly two miles south-east of the centre of Oxford, and is accessible either by walking along a riverside path or, by car, from the Iffley Road, the A4158.

St Mary the Virgin has the (not altogether deserved) reputation of being one of the best-preserved twelfth century village churches in England. Although the church is predominantly Romanesque, there are innovative indications of the developing Gothic style. It is situated in Iffley village, on the bank of the River Thames, close by the weir and lock. You can walk there from central Oxford, which is about two miles away via a footpath along the river.

The simple church plan of an aisleless nave, central tower and chancel is preserved. The east end has been lengthened, and this may have resulted in the destruction of an apse. The church was built in 1170–80 and it is attributed to the St Remy family who held the manor of Iffley at that time. The font of black marble is also late twelfth century.

The church has recently and controversially been restored (1975–84) and the renewed honey-coloured Oxfordshire stone is most striking. The church is richly ornamented, both internally and externally. The west front with its fine doorway is particularly remarkable and includes signs of the Zodiac and symbols of the Evangelists; the capitals of the south doorway show two horsemen fighting, a centaur suckling her young, and Samson with the lion.

This partly restored doorway at Iffley displays two typically Norman decorative motifs, the inner zigzags and the outer animal-heads: while a capital (right) demonstrates the difficulties centaurs experienced in suckling their young.

The granting of lands in England to the abbeys of France was common in the century following the Conquest, as a reward for both spiritual and temporal support. Isleham was a possession of the Benedictine house of St Jacut-sur-Mer, in Brittany, and is an excellent example of the small-scale churches of such "alien priories". The herring-bone masonry is characteristic of early Norman work and the structure is of great simplicity within. Both chancel and apse are without ornament, except for scallop-carved capitals on the chancel arch. Three plain windows light the apse, which is projected east of the chancel by an unbroken wall.

ISLEHAM PRIORY
Cambridgeshire
OS 143 TL 638744
Isleham is midway between Newmarket and Ely, and can be reached by turning eastward off the A142 between these places at Soham. The barn-like priory, clearly labelled, is in the middle of the village, and should not be confused with the huge and splendid medieval parish church, which is also well worth a visit.

The semi-circular apse at the east end of the Isleham Priory church, re-roofed after the Reformation for use as a village barn.

This Augustinian abbey was founded as a priory by King David I of Scotland (1124–53) in 1138, and promoted to an abbey by 1152. It was established by canons from the Abbey of St Quentin near Beauvais in France, and was the only Augustinian house in the Borders. The canons were significantly more community orientated than other orders (apart from the Premonstratensians at Dryburgh), and although the Cistercian house at Melrose was wealthier, Jedburgh became the most politically influential of the Border abbeys.

The abbey, built of the local pink sand-stone, occupies a beautiful setting, and when approached from the south presents an impressive view: the ruined church stands out above the excavated foundations of the cloisters and domestic ranges, which are terraced into the steep river bank of the Teviot. The town, built of predominantly grey limestone, lies up behind the abbey.

The whole church was finished by c.1220, when work was begun on the cloisters and domestic ranges, to the south. In the south wall of the church the twelfth century east processional door survives, and the west processional door has been well restored with

JEDBURGH ABBEY Borders
OS 74 NT 650204
The abbey is in the centre of Jedburgh, which is fifty-six miles south-east of Edinburgh, on the A68: all around is the beautiful border country, with its profusion of medieval monastic remains and fortified tower houses.

59

the same decoration. At the extreme east end (the presbytery) the style of architecture, whereby the massive Norman pillars are taken up high enough to envelop the triforium or upper arch, is unique in Scotland and rare in England.

Despite its political importance, Jedburgh suffered during the border campaigns between the English and the Scots, and was plundered so badly in 1297 that it was reported as uninhabitable. In the fifteenth century it was again badly damaged, and finally lay in ruins in 1545 after an attack by the Earl of Hertford. At this point the claustral buildings were largely robbed of stone, although the church remained in use as the parish church until 1857.

See **Romsey.**

Jedburgh Abbey church seen from the east end, with the sixteenth-century tower rising above the ruined Norman choir: the transept on the right has become a private chapel, while its twin to the left has vanished.

KENILWORTH CASTLE
Warwickshire
OS 140 SP 279723
Kenilworth is half-way between Coventry and the picturesque town of Warwick, on the A429: the castle is set in pleasant parkland on the southern edge of the town, with the attractive houses of Castle Green by its gate. The church and abbey are off the High Street.

The imposing ruins of Kenilworth epitomize the English castle with its mixture of fortification and domestic apartments, but it is only the formidable central keep which is of Norman date. Originally there may well have been a motte and bailey castle here, but if it existed this is now totally covered by the massive stone keep. One of the most striking features at Kenilworth is the high sloping plinth covering the lower part of the keep walls. This acted not only as a substantial foundation for the building, but also as a deterrent to would-be besiegers who hoped to tunnel through the base of the keep walls. The keep (which has angled turrets like so many others) was entered at first floor level. Elsewhere in the castle subsequent alterations, notably those by Queen Elizabeth's favourite Robert, Earl of Leicester, have removed virtually all trace of Norman work.

About fifty years after the Norman Conquest Henry I gave the Royal manor of Stoneleigh, which included Kenilworth, to his chamberlain Geoffrey de Clinton. Geoffrey founded a priory at Kenilworth, which later became an abbey, and whose ruins lie next to the parish church, with its fine Norman door. In order to provide them with fish for Fridays, Clinton allowed the monks to fish on Thursdays with boats and net in the waters beside his new castle and park. Kenilworth features frequently in the pages of English history.

The juxtaposition of a fine castle with a walled town makes Kidwelly one of the most interesting of the Norman settlements in western Wales. Built on the estuary of the river Gwendraeth, Kidwelly protected the main Norman road of the coastal plain, while the navigable river enabled the defenders to maintain a line of communication even when surrounded by land.

The original castle was built between 1106 and 1115, and the semi-circular moat and the rampart under the later curtain wall have been shown archaeologically to date from this period. Only fragments of Norman masonry survive, having been re-used in the extensive thirteenth century rebuilding, but the plan of castle and town has remained unaltered for nearly 900 years and can be seen with great clarity today. The settlement consists of two parts: on the west bank is the castle and the defended town, with its own wall: while on the other side of the river lies the priory church and a 'new' town that was deliberately planted in its shadow. The existence of St Mary's priory, founded before 1115, provides an example of how the Normans tackled the problems of Marcher settlement. The alien monks who were introduced were intended to provide a counterpoise to the anti-Norman sentiments of the native monasteries, as well as a stimulus to the development of the town.

KIDWELLY Dyfed
OS 159 SN 409071
Kidwelly stands on the south-west coast of Wales, twenty-four miles west of Swansea via the M4, the A4138 to Llanelli, and the A484.

Between 1122 and 1130, Walter L'Espec, the lord of Helmsley and friend of Henry I, founded this priory for Augustinian canons. The Austin canons or "black canons" lived a communal monastic life, following a rule based upon the letters of St Augustine of Hippo; the order was first established in England in c.1100.

The influence of the founder is clearly seen here. Walter installed his uncle as the first prior, and may well have been the prime mover behind the desire of some of the canons to join the Cistercian order through affiliation with Rievaulx (a house founded by Walter in 1131): but the proposal did not materialise.

Most of what is visible today belongs to the thirteenth century, including the fine gatehouse which is executed in exuberant Decorated style. Of the original mid twelfth century building programme, only the south wall of the nave, part of the west and south walls of the south transept and the slype or passage adjoining it outside remain. The north transept, the north nave and the western end of the church are all of the later Norman rebuild during the 1180s.

The monastery was dissolved in 1539 and fragments of monastic masonry may be seen in houses in the immediate vicinity of the priory. Kirkham priory is beautifully sited in the Derwent valley, with fine trees all round.

KIRKHAM PRIORY
North Yorkshire
OS 100 SE 737656
The priory is just off the A64(T) York-Scarborough road, from which it is signposted, five miles south-west of Malton and seventeen miles north-east of York. A few miles to the west are Sheriff Hutton, with massive ruins of a late medieval castle: and the palatial stately home of Castle Howard.

Kirstall Abbey is by far the most complete of the simple early Cistercian monasteries. Its buildings survive to a great height and little imagination is required to picture the monastic complex as it was in the twelfth century. Of particular note are the buildings around the cloister, all of which belong to the period 1152–1190. The abbey was founded in c.1152 by a colony from Fountains Abbey. The powerful northern baron Henry de Lacy of Pontefract not only helped the monks acquire the forty acre site by the banks of the River Aire from William of Poitou, but was also an active supporter during the construction of the abbey buildings.

The abbey church is characterised by the simplicity of its decoration. The crossing tower dominates the ruined church, but only its lower courses below the lantern are Norman: for the early Cistercians were forbidden by their constitution from such displays of pride as high towers, and it was only in 1509–28 that the tower was heightened. Simplicity is also found in the carvings around the windows and in the plain, pointed nave arches and round-headed doorways. The one exception is the impressive west door

KIRKSTALL ABBEY
Leeds, West Yorkshire
OS 104 SE 260361
The notably rewarding abbey is in the outer suburbs of Leeds, three miles north-west of the city centre and just off the A65 Leeds–Skipton road. For the traveller coming from the north, east or west, it is best reached via the Leeds by-pass ring road, turning towards the city centre on the A65. The gatehouse contains a most interesting folk museum.

The west door to the church, virtually the only elaborately decorated portion of the austere Cistercian abbey of Kirkstall.

with its chevron decoration and five recessed arches. The rib-vaulting in the chancel and nave is one of the architectural conundrums of the site. Does it derive from French or Anglo-Norman models? Opinion now favours the latter, tracing the inspiration from the Norman cathedral at Durham (c.1095) rather than from the French St Denis (c.1140). Insights into conventual worship are provided by the nave and choir, which are eight bays long to accommodate the Sunday processions of the community. The south side of the south transept contains the night doorway at first-floor level, leading from the

dormitories via the long vanished night-stairs, which were built of wood. Through this door the monks would have filed for the night services of Nocturns and Matins.

Leaving the church by the door just west of the south transept and moving round the cloister in a clockwise direction, we come to the chapter house. This is of two periods, the west part with its two wide archways giving access from the cloister being Norman, while the east part belongs to the late thirteenth century. Further round the cloister, the parlour, warming house, refectory and kitchen are all Norman in date.

Markedly restrained Norman carving round the entrance arches of Kirkstall's chapter house.

LEWES East Sussex
OS 198 TQ 415101

The picturesque hilltop town of Lewes is eight miles north-east of Brighton, via the A27, and fifty-one miles south of London. The castle, high up, dominates the town: the somewhat scanty remains of the priory lie at the foot of the hill to the south, being reached from Cockshut Road; while the remains of the priory gate, and St John's church with Warenne's tomb, are in Southover High Street.

Lewes was already a fortified town, with two Saxon mints, long before the Norman Conquest: and as such it was the head of one of the administrative areas, or "rapes", into which Sussex was then divided. After 1066, King William gave each rape to one of his principal barons, and Lewes went to William of Warenne, who soon afterwards built a great castle there. This was a link in the chain of south coast Norman fortresses, designed to protect the routes between England and Normandy: but it was attacked only once in its history, during the Battle of Lewes in 1264, and was abandoned after the last of the Warennes died in 1347.

Like most early Norman strongholds, Lewes is a motte and bailey castle, although it is unusual in having (like Lincoln) not one but two mottes, one at each end of the bailey: both are still visible today, although the eastern one is behind the bowling green and

covered in scrub. The remains of the curtain wall linking the mottes also survive, showing evidence of early Norman herring-bone masonry: and so too does the late eleventh century rectangular gatehouse, behind the mighty fourteenth century barbican or outer gate, with its round towers.

But Warenne was not merely a soldier. Travelling with his wife Gundrada on pilgrimage to Rome in 1075, he stayed at the famous abbey of Cluny in Burgundy: and on his return he founded at Lewes the first English priory of the Cluniac order, on the flat land south of the town hill. Comparatively little of this now remains, but the tombs of Warenne and Gundrada are still to be seen at the nearby church of St John the Baptist, Southover, which was once the guest-house outside the priory gate.
See **Lincoln.**

Lincoln arguably possesses the finest collection of medieval architecture in the country, and the city owes its outstanding skyline to its Norman cathedral, sharing its prominent hill-top position with the castle which William the Conqueror built in 1068 on his return from York. William sited his castle within a corner of the surviving Roman defences, and according to the Domesday Book houses were levelled to make way for it. The castle plan survives largely unaltered, and consists of a curtain wall of eleventh century date in the lower portion, defending the inner ward on the north, west and east sides, while to the south its two mottes dominate the ground which slopes steeply to the River Witham below. The mound at the south-east corner of the castle has a square tower, the lower portion of which is probably Norman, and was probably the original motte of the Conqueror's castle. The western mound, the larger of the two, appears to have been added later and is surmounted by a twelfth century shell keep known as the Lucy Tower.

The castle walls provide an excellent vantage point for viewing the cathedral, especially the Norman west front which is framed within magnificent thirteenth century work. Unfortunately, this section of the west front is the only significant surviving element of the first cathedral built by Bishop Remigius. Remigius contributed financially to the cost of William's invasion force and was rewarded with the English bishopric of Dorchester-on-Thames near Oxford, but with the decision at the Council of Windsor in 1072 that bishops should have their headquarters in fortified towns rather than villages, Remigius was encouraged to move to Lincoln.

Fire in 1141 and earthquake in 1185 between them destroyed most of the original Norman cathedral, and in part human error was to blame as well. The fire destroyed the original wooden roof; and Bishop Alexander, in the twelfth century, ordered a roof of vaulted stone which was heavier than the Norman nave walls were designed to bear. As a result the earthquake of 1185 reduced most of the structure to rubble, and the building which survives is the Early English gem – which John Ruskin considered 'out and out the most precious piece of architecture in the British Isles and roughly speaking worth any two other cathedrals we have'.

In addition to the castle and cathedral, Lincoln has one of the finest collections of Norman domestic architecture in the country. The "Jew's House", in the Strait retains a number of the original Norman features on the street frontage: a ground floor doorway with decorated capitals; a Romanesque arch supporting the chimney of a fireplace in the first floor chamber; and both windows on the first floor. "Aaron the Jew's House" on Steep Hill appears to fit the tradition of a certain Aaron who lived in Lincoln during 1166–86. The main doorway here has a round-headed arch with a chimney buttress above, and the

first floor window to the south is a reset and restored Norman window discovered in pieces in a ground floor recess during general restoration in 1878.

To the south of the city centre St Mary's Guildhall, with its west range fronting onto the High Street and large arched doorway measuring some sixteen by fourteen feet across, provides a fine example of later twelfth century town architecture. The east range appears to be contemporary at first sight, but is in fact of a much later date, though faithfully copying the Norman style.

LINCOLN Lincolnshire
OS 121 SK 975719
Lincoln is 131 miles north of London, via the A1 and A46. The cathedral dominates not only the city but the whole surrounding area, and just opposite its west gate is the castle, which was long used as a gaol and displays a horrifying prison chapel and the pitiful graves of prisoners (within the Lucy Tower on the western motte). Aaron the Jew's House and the Jew's House are both on the steep hill leading down from the castle and cathedral into the city centre, and St Mary's Guildhall is much further south on the High Street, near a railway crossing and next to St Peter-at-Gowts church with its Saxon tower. There is also much else to see in Lincoln, and the Museum of Lincolnshire Life in Burton Road is especially worth a visit.

Lincoln's two rare and precious Norman town houses, both of the later twelfth century. The so-called "Jew's House" has a sculpted doorway with chimney breast above: while "Aaron the Jew's House", below, has a fine two-light window lighting its main hall.

LINDISFARNE PRIORY
Northumberland
OS 75 NU 126418

Holy Island is sixteen miles south of Berwick-on-Tweed, and is reached by turning east off the main A1 five miles north of Belford, onto a well-signposted minor road. Prominently displayed tide-tables indicate the times when it is possible to drive across the causeway: and these should also be checked to avoid the possibility of being marooned on the island until the next low tide. Should this occur, however, there is a great deal to see, and several hotels and cafés.

Weathered by centuries of sea winds, the incised decoration on this pillar recalls Lindisfarne Priory's links with the Durham mother-house. Right, the "rainbow arch" once supported the vault of a now-vanished tower.

This most atmospheric of monastic ruins stands on Holy Island, off the Northumberland coast and accessible across a causeway only at low tide. The island is an outcrop of the hard rock called the Whin Sill, surrounded by broad expanses of tidal flats: and the priory is romantically set against a backdrop of sea and fishing boats, with Lindisfarne Castle clinging to its crag beyond. Also called Lindisfarne, the place received its name of Holy Island from the Normans, but it was sacred long before their coming. For here, in 634, St Aidan established a community of monks from Iona, and set out from this base to convert the pagan Northumbrians: and here, some fifty years later, the miracle-working hermit bishop St Cuthbert died and was buried. In the early Anglo-Saxon period, indeed, the island was both a spiritual powerhouse and a great European centre of learning: but its exposed position made it an easy prey to Viking raids, and in 875 the monks were forced to flee with St Cuthbert's hallowed bones, which after many wanderings found their resting place in Durham Cathedral.

Lindisfarne, therefore, had a special significance for the Durham community: and in 1083 Bishop William of St Calais despatched a party of Durham monks to re-establish the monastery as a dependent offshoot of the cathedral priory. They began to build ten years later and finished in about 1140, so that the work here is roughly contemporary with that at Durham Cathedral: and not surprisingly there are many similarities of architectural style between the two churches, notably the zig-zag carved pillars which appear in both places.

The priory church is built of dark red Goswick sandstone, now much weathered and etched with strange twisted patterns by the continual wind from the sea. It is entered by a richly ornamented door in the typically Norman west front: whose top storey, however, has not windows but loopholes for crossbows – a reminder, like the fortified wall round the extensive monastic buildings to the south, that Lindisfarne's monks could never relax their vigilance against sea-raiders. Moving eastwards to the centre of the church, past the stumps of zig-zag carved nave pillars, the traveller reaches the most striking feature of the whole ruin: the 'rainbow arch', a solitary rib of the tower vault, springing diagonally between two of the massive pillars which once supported the long-fallen central tower itself. Beyond are the still substantial walls of the mid twelfth century chancel.

The monastic buildings, the site museum, and the adjacent thirteenth century parish church of St Mary are also worth investigating: as is nearby Lindisfarne Castle – a sixteenth century fort partly constructed with stones from the priory, and imaginatively rebuilt by the Edwardian architect Lutyens. *See* **Durham.**

The Castles of the Norman Conquest

"He caused castles to be built
Which were a heavy burden to the poor
A stern man was the king"

The Anglo-Saxon Chronicle, 1087

"They filled the whole land with these castles . . and when the castles
were built, they filled them with devils and wicked men"

The Anglo-Saxon Chronicle, 1137

For the Anglo-Saxon Chronicler and his contemporaries, as for subsequent generations up until the present, the Normans and their castles
are inseparable. Before the Norman Conquest, indeed, castles as such
were virtually unknown in England: and the few that did exist (like
Richard's Castle in Herefordshire) were the work of the Norman knights
who came to England during the 1050s to serve King Edward the Confessor. Fortifications of other kinds were, of course, familiar to the Anglo-
Saxons. But these were invariably intended to protect whole communi-
ties, like the *burhs* or fortress-towns founded by Alfred and his descendants as bastions against the Vikings: and the idea of "private" strongholds
– for the castle is best defined as a strongly fortified residence belonging
to one man, be he king or baron – was an alien and even a repugnant
one to the English. Thus, reported the Anglo-Norman writer Ordericus
Vitalis, "the fortresses which the French call castles were very rare in
England: and for this reason the English (though brave and warlike)
were unable to resist their enemies".

These enemies, the invading Normans, were the products of a very
different tradition. For castles had been known in France for well over

a century before 1066 – in 1027 the Conqueror himself had been born in one, at Falaise – and indeed it seems probable that the concept of the private fortress had actually originated there. These early French castles (like the oldest surviving example, built at Doué-la-Fontaine in Anjou in about 950) frequently took the form of stone-built rectangular "keeps", also called "great towers" (though they might be broader than they were high): and it was this style that the Normans were to adopt for the largest and most imposing of their English fortresses. But mighty keeps like the White Tower of London and Colchester (and later Rochester, Norwich, and Dover) might take long years to build, and were necessarily the product of reasonably settled conditions: and what the Normans needed during the campaigns of the Conquest – or whenever they were expanding their power into potentially hostile territory – were strongholds which could be raised as quickly as possible, but yet which would provide as secure as possible a base for operations.

By far the most commonly-occurring type of early Norman fortress, then, was the simple "motte and bailey" castle. Its essential feature, the motte, was a conical and flat-topped earthen mound, generally constructed by digging a more or less circular ditch and casting the excavated earth inwards, rather in the manner of a sand-castle. Extra material (often rammed-down alternate layers of earth and stones) could then be added to the mound, which might measure forty feet or more in height and be a great deal larger in diameter. The base of the motte being already defended by the ditch, its flat top would be fortified with a timber palisade of sharpened stakes, within which was often built a wooden tower, sometimes raised on stilts for additional security and increased field of fire.

This motte was the defensive core of the castle, while its tower frequently accommodated the garrison commander. Its cramped top, however, would normally be too small to allow sufficient room for necessities like stores and horses – the Normans being first and foremost cavalrymen: and in order to provide protection for these (and perhaps for a hall and a chapel) a fortified enclosure called the "bailey" would be constructed at the foot of the mound, complete with its own ditch, bank and palisade. Sometimes the bailey entirely surrounded the motte, but more often the motte stood on its periphery: and larger castles might have two or more baileys ranged round the motte, or even (as at Lewes and Lincoln) two mottes with a bailey between them.

Whether the motte and bailey castle was already a well-established type of fortification in pre-1066 Normandy, or whether it first came to prominence in response to the needs of the invasion campaigns, remains a matter for controversy. But certainly a number of such strongholds are depicted in the near-contemporary Bayeux Tapestry, among these being the very first example raised in Britain, the Conqueror's motte at Hastings. This, according to the chroniclers, was built in a mere fifteen days: and even allowing for some exaggeration it is clear that a motte and bailey castle could be constructed very speedily – generally, of course, by gangs of conscripted native labourers. Hundreds of these fortresses, indeed, sprung up during the consolidation of Norman control over England; and hundreds more (in fact, the densest concentration of them in Britain) mark the progress of the more gradual Norman infiltration of Wales and the Welsh borders.

Where these castles continued in use for only a year or two before the invaders moved on, they rarely developed anything beyond simple earth and timber defences: but in the castles they built to permanently overawe a town or control some strategic road or river-crossing, the Normans soon discovered the need for stronger and more sophisticated fortifications. Even in peacetime, for example, weathering caused ditches to subside and timber towers and palisades to rot, while in time of war wooden castles were extremely and dangerously vulnerable to attack by fire. Very soon after the Conquest, therefore, the timber defences of many castles were being rebuilt in stone.

This process generally began on the motte, whose palisade might be replaced by a masonry ring-wall, thus creating a "shell-keep" like those at Carisbrooke and Totnes: alternatively, a stone keep might be directly substituted for a motte-top wooden tower, though more often the mound would prove too uncertain a foundation for such a weighty building, which would therefore have to be built at ground level – as, for instance, at Clun. In time, too, the wooden defences of the bailey came also to be rebuilt in stone, often beginning with the gate-house: and later still plain stone bailey walls (like those at White Castle) were additionally protected by protruding towers, which allowed the garrison to direct a murderous flanking fire at attackers undermining the base of the wall or attempting to scale it.

In some cases, of course, castles were built in stone from the outset: and whether or not it succeeds an earlier motte and bailey structure, undoubtedly the most impressive feature of the greater Norman castle is its mighty rectangular stone keep. Squat and four-square or high and tower-like, grimly plain or richly decorated like Norwich and Castle Rising, such "fortress-palaces" (as a contemporary called the White Tower) remain almost as awesome today as when they were built – to quote another contemporary – as "the bones of the kingdom". Even here, however, new developments were in train during the mid and later twelfth century, as castle builders strove to solve the problem of right-angled corners – vulnerable both to undermining and the battering of siege-engines – by building polygonal or round keeps (as at Tretower) or semi-circular towers on bailey walls (like those at Dover). Castle defences, indeed, were to become steadily more and more complex as the Middle Ages progressed: yet comparatively few entirely new castles would be raised after the Norman period. For it was the Normans above all who "filled the whole land with castles", leaving them as dramatic proof of their determination to cow the conquered English and maintain their grip on their newly-won land.

See **The Normans; Norman Architecture.**

LLANSTEPHAN CASTLE
Dyfed
OS 159 SN 351101

Llanstephan Castle rises above a sandy beach in a picturesque part of the south Wales coast: it is seven miles south-west of Carmarthen via the B4312.

With stunning views over Carmarthen Bay, this early twelfth century castle stands in a well-defended position high on a ridge above the confluence of the Tywi and Taf rivers. Access is not easy even today, the approach being up a rough track. However, the castle was stormed by a Welsh force in 1136 and by 1192 had been extensively refortified against continuing attacks.

Originally there was an inner ring-work associated with the keep. The outer defence is in the form of a double ditch which has been much levelled. Nevertheless, the west part of the great stone curtain wall remains, as does the gatehouse tower, remodelled in the late twelfth and early thirteenth centuries.

An interesting detail is the bar-hole in the original curtain wall, which would have served to bolt the timber gate. Its position suggests that the present gatehouse tower superseded an earlier building.

The towers of Llanstephan Castle, seen across Carmarthen Bay.

TOWER OF LONDON London
OS 176 TQ 336805

The Tower stands by the Thames, to the east of St Paul's Cathedral and the old City of London: it is, of course, one of the great showpieces of Britain, with its famous Yeoman Warders, ravens, Crown Jewels and (for the ghoulish) the site of the block where so many famous prisoners perished.

A dozen years after the Norman Conquest, work began on a great stone keep – built on a scale not attempted in Britain since Roman times – to replace the campaign fort hastily constructed in a corner of London's Roman defences at the time of King William's coronation. This was the White Tower, the original "tower of London", whose formidable presence was intended to overawe the turbulent citizens, and which today stands at the heart of the much-expanded fortress named after it. So called from the medieval practice of plaster-rendering its exterior walls, its construction (like that of Colchester Castle,

Rochester Cathedral, and several other great early Norman buildings) was supervised by the architect-bishop Gundulf: and it has been plausibly suggested that he based its design on the now-vanished palace of the Dukes of Normandy at Rouen. Contemporaries, indeed, referred to it as "a fortified palace": and it is not only the earliest stone keep in England, but also (with the single exception of Colchester) the largest, well over a hundred feet square and ninety feet high.

Although the White Tower appears rectangular, no two sides of it are in fact the same length. Its external walls, fifteen feet thick at their base, are mainly of Kentish ragstone, but the neatly dressed stones at the corners and around the windows were brought from Caen, in the Normans' home duchy: only two of the present windows, however (those on the top storey of the keep's southern face, at its extreme western end) are original, the remainder being restorations.

Like many other Norman keeps, the White Tower was entered via a wooden stairway (once protected by a now-demolished fore-building) to the first floor, the ground floor or basement being used for storage and the imprisonment, over the centuries, of genera-tions of hapless captives. The principal living accommodation, however, was on the first and second floors, where a number of orig-inal Norman fireplaces and garderobe-lavatories still survive: and the king himself normally lodged on the second floor, wor-shipping in the austere and dignified chapel of St John the Baptist there. This chapel, whose semi-circular apse accounts for the rounded bulge in the keep's plan, is one of the most evocative buildings in all Norman England: and though simple crosses carved on its pillar capitals are virtually its only decoration, the rhythm of its massive arches is almost overwhelmingly impressive.

For all its great strength, the White Tower was not intended to stand alone: and by 1097, according to the Anglo-Saxon Chron-icle, "sorely oppressed" English conscripts from all the shires near London had begun to construct a stone wall around it. Very little survives of this early Norman wall, though the Bell Tower (one of the earliest polygonal wall towers in Britain) and an adjacent stretch of the defences date from the late twelfth cen-tury: while later still the Norman keep was given first an inner and then an outer bailey, both studded with round towers, until it be-came the centre of a vast concentric fortress, perhaps the strongest in all medieval Eng-land. But despite all this expansion, it is the White Tower which still dominates the whole complex, and this dominance can best be appreciated from a distance, looking from Tower Hill or (for the more adventurous) from the elevated vantage point of Tower Bridge's upper walkway. It must, however,

also be inspected at close quarters; and it now has the added attraction of housing an incomparable collection of arms and armour. See **Castles of the Norman Conquest.**

The south-facing elevation of the White Tower.

Ludlow castle was one of the great fortresses of the Norman Marcher barons. In the late twelfth century Roger de Lacy built there a massive gatehouse-cum-keep, surrounded by a rock cut ditch and perched on a cliff over-looking a bend of the River Teme in southern Shropshire. Later the arrangements of the castle were changed so that the gatehouse became exclusively a keep, and the original Norman entrance was blocked up. The outlines of it, however, can still clearly be seen on the southern side of this massive edifice. Within the original bailey there is a further surprise, the tall circular nave of a chapel

dated to about 1130, which can be compared to the church of Saint Sepulchre in Cam-bridge. The exterior doorway has a little decoration in the early Norman tradition, and some chevron ornament can be identified on the arches of the wall seating arcades on the interior. This building, although now roofless and bereft of its attached rectangular chancel, is a truly remarkable survival.

A new town was laid out to a regular plan within the shadow of the Norman castle, and the regular grid chequer of the original streets can still be identified on the ground today. Ludlow is in fact a classic early medieval

LUDLOW Shropshire
OS 138 SO 508746
The most attractive and interesting town of Ludlow is twenty-eight miles south of Shrewsbury, on the A49. Apart from the easily-found castle, the great medieval church of St Lawrence (the largest in the county) is worth a visit, particularly for its fifteenth century carved misericords under the choir seats: while the maze of streets in the town centre display many fine timber-framed houses, notably the Feathers Inn and the Bull Hotel in the Bull Ring.

planned town, designed principally to attract the trade which could flourish under the protection of the nearby castle. It was one of the most successful of the Norman town plantations, and as the threat of Welsh Marcher warfare moved westwards, became increasingly prosperous as a centre of the wool trade.

See **Church of the Holy Sepulchre, Cambridge.**

The curious circular nave of Ludlow Castle's chapel, with arched niches for the congregation who sat on the stone bench round the wall.

The village and castle of Lydford occupy an attractive location overlooking the river Lyd, on the western edge of Dartmoor. This site was chosen by Alfred for a fortification, and as one of the four Devon *burhs* it became an important administrative centre in the late Saxon period. The Domesday Book records that forty houses were laid waste within the town (which may indicate the building of an early castle here) and an enormous square keep still survives, partly buried by an earthen mound. This was probably built in about 1195 as a prison for the administrative courts of the local "stannaries" (tin-mining districts) and of the royal forest of Dartmoor: and certainly the castle served as both court and prison throughout the middle ages and up until the seventeenth century, "Lydford Law" being notorious for its summary punishments:

> "I oft have heard of Lydford law
> How in the morn they hang and draw
> And sit in judgement after".

The castle at Lydford thus serves as a reminder not only of Norman military might but also of their intense involvement in profitable economic enterprises like tin-mining.

LYDFORD Devon
OS 191 SX 510848
Lydford is seven miles north of Tavistock, just west of the A386.

The monastery at Malmesbury was founded in the mid seventh century by the Irish monk Maeldulph, and then refounded for Benedictine monks in the late tenth century. The abbey buildings were burnt down in 1042 and rebuilt somewhere in the latter half of the twelfth century. The present Norman building dates from around 1160–1175, and was begun after the death of Bishop Roger of Old Salisbury, builder of the Castles at Sherborne (Dorset) and Old Sarum (Wiltshire), and holder of Malmesbury from 1118 until his demise.

The present church is only a fragment of the original abbey church, which had transepts, a tall central spire and a western tower. All that is left today is the nave with aisles, but the south porch contains some of the very finest Norman sculpture in Britain. It consists of two doorways, the outer of which is similar to the west door at Iffley (Oxford) in having eight decorated bands around the entrance. The inner door has three bands and a tympanum over the top, depicting Christ in Majesty. On the side walls of the porch are two more tympana, each containing six Apostles with an angel above each of them. It is possible that the sculptures of the porch are copied from French examples, perhaps from Autun Cathedral in Burgundy. This use of tympana on the side walls of the porch is most unusual in England, but is known on Romanesque churches in south-west France. There are, however, similar sculptures on the west front of Lincoln Cathedral, which may also have influenced the masons of Malmesbury.

See **Iffley Church.**

MALMESBURY Wiltshire
OS 173 ST 933874
The pleasant hill town of Malmesbury is sixteen miles west of Swindon, and can be reached via junction 16 of the M4 motorway and the B9042. Visitors should also notice the fine market cross by the abbey gateway, built in about 1500 "for poor folks to stand dry when the rain cometh".

Despite its unfortunate exterior appearance, with a tithe-barn close to the west front, the church of St Michael and St Mary has one of the most impressive and exciting Norman interiors in England. Approaching the two-towered west facade from Church Street, it is apparent that the towers were never completed. Nevertheless, the central door of the west front, with its elaborate sculptural decoration, conveys an impression of the intended grandeur of a facade which is without parallel in Norman parish churches.

Probably the plan of the church (towered facade, aisled six-bay nave and transepts, with a central tower, chancel and apse) was devised before 1100, even though the details of the stonework seem closer to twelfth century styles. Such an imposing plan is believed to have its origin in the tenth and eleventh century German and Carolingian Romanesque tradition.

On the interior of the west front, there is a great deal of interest to see. Three groin-vaulted rooms span the interior, with the central one opening into the nave under a broad arch. Above this is a gallery, itself open to the nave. Such an arrangement is unique in England.

Looking along the length of the nave, above the heavily chevroned arches, on the north side can be seen an upper wall-passage with openings towards the centre. Probably this arrangement also once existed on the south side. It is a motif common enough in cathedrals or great monastic churches, but extraordinary in a parish church: and the grandeur of the great transept crossing is also rare in such a location. This has arches on all four sides, and on the eastern arch are good carvings of grotesques and human figures to vary the flat foliage of the capitals. Inside the crossing tower, three tiers of openings rise above the arches. The lower tier opens into the nave, while the higher ones open into an upper storey of the chancel. This very unusual arrangement contributes to the vivid sense of a buiding almost bursting with the high ambition of its unknown architect.

Notable, too, are the fourteenth-century wall paintings on the piers supporting the tower. On the north-west pier devils perch on the backs of two women, and on the opposite wall are episodes from the Crucifixion story.

MELBOURNE CHURCH
Derbyshire
OS 128 SK 389250
Melbourne is seven and a half miles south-east of Derby, via the A514: it also possesses the remains of a medieval castle, and a mile or so to the east is the hilltop church of Breedon-on-the-Hill, with its unique collection of Anglo-Saxon sculpture.

Melrose Abbey, Scotland's finest monastic ruin.

MELROSE ABBEY Borders
OS 73 NT 550343
Melrose, dominated by the triple peaks of the Eildon Hills, is forty miles south of Edinburgh, via the A7 or the A68. Dryburgh Abbey is nearby, and all around is the beautiful wooded countryside of the Borders.

The abbey occupies a beautiful location on the south bank of the River Tweed. It was colonised by monks from the Cistercian house at Rievaulx in 1136, who at first settled at Old Melrose, on the site of an earlier Saxon monastery. Finding that site unsuitable, however, they shortly afterwards moved three miles upstream to a place then called Little Fordell, now Melrose itself.

The abbey was very richly endowed in the twelfth and thirteenth centuries and became one of the wealthiest in Scotland. Its principal revenue came from cattle and sheep and the trading of wool and skins: the abbey was given houses and land in Berwick, Scotland's major port on the east coast, and received trading protection from the Count of Flanders in time of war. The monks also had extensive estates with farms, fisheries, salt marshes and a peat moss for fuel, and property in several other burghs.

Very little remains of the twelfth century Norman buildings, as the church was almost entirely rebuilt in the fifteenth and sixteenth centuries, and little more than the foundations of the cloisters and domestic buildings survive. But the ruins of the later church, unrivalled in Scotland and among the most spectacular monastic remains in Britain, are well worth a visit. Standing to their full height in many places, they are particularly remarkable for their great traceried windows and profusion of delightful wall-carvings, whose subjects range from the Crucifixion to a bagpipe-playing pig. Melrose was also a favourite abbey of the Scots royal house, and beneath its chapter house lies a casket containing the heart of King Robert the Bruce.

A nunnery was founded at the eastern end of Wenlock Edge by the Saxon saint Milburga at the end of the seventh century: and a second foundation for men was made by Earl Leofric of Mercia and his famous wife Lady Godiva in about 1050. After the Conquest Roger de Montgomery incorporated the property of Leofric's church in his foundation for Cluniac monks from La Charité-sur-Loire. It remained an alien priory until 1395, when along with other Cluniac institutions it broke its links with the French mother house. Wenlock was a prosperous and important monastic establishment, and despite economic vicissitudes it generally prospered. This prosperity can be seen even in the ruins, now magnificently displayed in a wooded setting.

Of the Norman period two masterpieces survive. The intersecting arcading in the chapter house represents some of the finest of its kind in the country, and the impressive figure sculpture in the lavatorium (or wash-house) in the centre of the cloister appears to be the work of the local Hereford School of masons. Close by, the prior's separate parish church of the Holy Trinity has a grand Norman nave and chancel plus a tower of about 1200 in the west wall: and also worthy of note are the very fine late fifteenth century infirmary and prior's lodging, now a private house.

MUCH WENLOCK PRIORY
Shropshire
OS 138 SO 625001
Much Wenlock is fourteen miles south-east of Shrewsbury via the A458, on the fringe of the hill country of Wenlock Edge. Nearby is Buildwas Abbey and the excellent Ironbridge Gorge Museum.

Above, the south transept of Much Wenlock Priory, with the cloister and round-arched entrance of the chapter house to the right. Right, one of the finest displays of Norman decoration in Britain, the intersecting blank arcades within the chapter house.

The Normans
and the English Church

The Norman Conquest of England heralded an era of great change in the English Church. The expedition was mounted with the blessing of Pope Alexander II in the spirit of a crusade, as the means by which an institution regarded by many as wayward and decadent might be brought back into line with Rome, and introduced to the recent reforms of the European Churches.

For Duke William, who wished to stress the legitimacy of his claim to the English throne as the nominee of Edward the Confessor, papal support for his enterprise was crucial: for it made the conquest of England lawful in the eyes of the Church, and encouraged the early submission of the English clergy. Their submission did not, however, guarantee their positions. Essentially a warrior, and completely illiterate himself, William valued learned Norman clerics such as Lanfranc of Bec highly as advisers, and as his agents in imposing Norman rule on his newly-won kingdom. Within four years of the Conquest, Lanfranc was made Archbishop of Canterbury, and he and William implemented a policy of such wholesale re-organisation of the English clergy, that by 1076 Wulfstan of Worcester was the only Saxon bishop to remain in office. By the early twelfth century the upper hierarchy of the English church had been re-staffed so comprehensively that William of Malmesbury was moved to exclaim:

"England has become a residence for foreigners and the property of aliens. At the present time there is no English earl nor bishop: strangers all, they prey upon the riches and vitals of England"

The Norman kings continued the existing policy of moving cathedrals from the old missionary centres to populous towns. Sherborne was moved to Old Sarum, Lichfield to Chester and Dorchester-on-Thames to Lincoln, to name but some of the changes made. With the creation of the new sees of Carlisle and Ely by Henry I, the Norman kings established the diocesan framework which stood for four hundred years, until the Reformation. The spate of building which accompanied this trend meant the eclipse of the outmoded style of Saxon architecture, and of minor arts such as metalwork and embroidery which had flourished before the Conquest.

Not only the buildings, but also the archaic liturgy and multiplicity of native saints of the Anglo-Saxon church were regarded with distrust and dislike by the Norman clerics. Lanfranc himself pondered:

"These Englishmen among whom we are living have set up for themselves certain saints whom they revere; but sometimes, when I turn over in my mind their own accounts of whom they were, I cannot help having doubts about the quality of their sanctity."

In the immediate wake of the Conquest, indeed, some Norman abbots went so far as to break up the tombs of their sainted English predecessors, and to subject the bones of English saints to ordeal by fire, only admitting those whose remains emerged intact from the flames to be possessed of genuine sanctity! By the twelfth century however, the early hostility toward the old Saxon saints had declined, probably as a result of a recog-

nition of their financial importance in attracting pilgrims.

Under the guidance of Lanfranc the administration of the English church was also remodelled along Norman lines. Having established the primacy of the see of Canterbury over that of York, the Archbishop proceeded to improve the structure of cathedral and diocesan administration. The hierarchies of a bishop aided by an archdeacon and rural deans in the diocese and a dean and chapter of monks or secular canons in the cathedral evolved, and with them, the characteristic English cathedral close of buildings needed to house them and provide a diocesan centre. The introduction of church councils meant the gradual imposition of stricter rules for the clergy, including celibacy, while criminal clerics were permitted to be tried in the church courts.

Quite apart from the re-organisation of the church, the Norman Conquest resulted in the accelerated spread of monasticism. The northern English monasteries had been devastated by continued Viking depredations during the ninth and tenth centuries, and in 1066 there were only fifty-two religious houses in England. By 1200 this figure had more than quadrupled through the influence of the new Norman aristocracy, who developed the tradition of clerical patronage existing in Normandy. Five major Benedictine houses (Chester, Colchester, Shrewsbury, Selby and Battle abbeys) were established by 1100, the latter two by William himself. During the early decades of the twelfth century, moreover, successive waves of monastic orders founded new houses in England, while the Benedictines spearheaded the revival with the establishment of St Mary's Abbey in York and Durham Priory in 1078 and 1083. The first Cluniac monastery was founded at Lewes (1078–82) by William Warenne. These orders were soon followed by the austere Cistercians, who followed a reformed Benedictine Rule. Their abbeys at Rievaulx and Fountains were founded in 1131 and 1132, and by 1167 Rievaulx had grown to a community of over six hundred monks and lay brothers.

The twelfth century also saw the diversification of monastic life in England with the influx of the Premonstratensian, Grandmontine and hermit-like Carthusian monastic orders; of regular canons such as the Augustinians; and of the military order of the Knights Templar. It likewise saw the foundation of the Gilbertine order; the only one during the whole of the Middle Ages to be founded in England by an Englishman, Gilbert of Sempringham.

Norham has a layout common to many Norman foundations, being a two-row village with a triangular market square, strung out between the castle and the church. Although the modern road is re-routed round the castle, it is clear that the main village street originally ran directly from the market place at the west end to the gates of the castle at the east end. The church is slightly offset, to the north-west of the market place.

In 1121 it is recorded that Bishop Flambard of Durham had a castle built here. It became the chief stronghold of this outlying part of the Durham estates, commanding one of the fords of the Tweed, and together with Berwick and Wark-upon-Tweed it guarded the eastern sector of the border with Scotland.

Although much rebuilt, Norham Castle is a classic Norman motte and bailey, with the twelfth century stone keep, west gate, and part of the curtain wall still standing. The rest of the walls date from the later medieval period. It is set on high ground on the south bank of the River Tweed, protected on the north and west by the steep river banks, and

NORHAM Northumberland
OS 74/75 NT 906474
Norham stands on the Tweed and the Anglo-Scottish border, seven miles south of Berwick-on-Tweed via the A698 and a minor road. A few miles to the south are two more border castles, Etal and Ford, and (at Branxton) the battlefield of Flodden (1513).

Norham Castle's sturdy rectangular keep, on its earlier motte, guarded a ford over the border river Tweed: within were three storeys of lodgings.

on the east by an artificially deepened ravine. The castle mound is further strengthened by a deep moat running round the south side, and it is likely that the present ditches of the inner and outer baileys correspond to those of Flambard's castle.

Norham was also an important religious site in the Saxon period, and its first stone church is said to have been founded in 830. The coffin of St Cuthbert was temporarily brought here from Lindisfarne by monks fleeing from Viking raiders: and the bodies of

St Coelwulf, king of Northumbria and later a monk, and of Gospatric the first earl of Northumberland, were also buried here.

The present building of St Cuthbert's church was begun in 1165, and the Norman sections surviving include the long chancel, the arches on the south side of the nave and the wall above them, three pillar bases on the north side of the nave, and the foundations of the side walls. There is some attractive decoration on the exterior of five of the windows in the south wall of the chancel.

77

Norwich is 114 miles north-east of London, via the M11 and A11. The castle and the cathedral are both easily found near the centre of the city: and among the many attractions which make Norwich one of the most fascinating English cities are no less than thirty-two medieval parish churches, mainly dating from the fourteenth and fifteenth centuries. The cathedral-like St Peter Mancroft, overlooking the market place, is the grandest of them all. The medieval-minded traveller should also see the St Peter Hungate Museum of Church Art, in picturesque Elm Hill; the Strangers' Hall Museum, in Charing Cross; St Andrew's Hall (once a friary church) in St Andrew's Plain; and the medieval walls which still surround the old city.

Above, Bishop Losinga's tombstone in the north transept of his cathedral at Norwich. Right, a forest of soaring pillars in the nave – like the mirror in the foreground – carries the traveller's eye heavenwards.

Norwich boasts two of Britain's finest Norman buildings, its castle and its cathedral. In origin, the castle is the earlier of the two, for a fortress was raised here very soon after the Conquest, nearly a hundred houses being destroyed to make room for it. It is sited on a natural hill, which was ditched and landscaped for additional security, and doubtless its first fortifications were the usual wooden palisade and timber tower. Then, probably quite early in the twelfth century, this last was replaced by a mighty stone keep, some ninety-five by ninety feet square and seventy feet high, and thus one of the very largest keeps in Norman England. But where most

such fortresses were functionally grim and plain-walled, the exterior walls of Norwich were almost entirely covered with lavish sculptural decoration: and though what we now see is the result of a complete refacing of the keep in 1833–9, it is known that this faithfully reproduced the original.

The keep's lowest storey is plain, broken only by the broad, flat buttresses which rise cleanly the whole height of the building: but above it rise serried tiers of blank arches, three tiers on the east and west faces and four on the north and south. On all four sides, too, appear round-headed single-light or columned two-light windows, though not in any

regular pattern. Entrance, as in most Norman keeps, was by steps to the first floor: and though the forebuilding which now covers these is relatively modern, the entrance portal itself is original (though incomplete) and is the most ornately decorated feature of the whole building. The capitals which support its arch are particularly fine, the most notable being one showing a swordsman and his hunting dog attacking their prey.

If, as is generally believed, the castle was built during the reign of Henry I (1100–1130), it must have been rising at much the same time as Norwich's other famous Norman building, the cathedral. For that great church (which like so many other English cathedrals was served until the Reformation by Benedictine monks) was begun by Bishop Herbert de Losinga in 1096, a year after he had transferred the seat of his East Anglian bishopric to Norwich from Thetford. By the time of his death in 1119, Losinga had finished the eastern and central parts of the church – the chancel, transepts, and part of the nave – and building continued westward under his successor Bishop Everard, so that by 1145 the cathedral was complete. Neither has it been substantially rebuilt since that time.

Like its contemporary at Durham, therefore, Norwich is among the most completely Norman of English cathedrals: but though the two buildings were constructed at almost precisely the same period, they are very dif-ferent in style. For while Durham conveys massive strength, Norwich gives a far lighter and more graceful impression, and it has been suggested that this is largely due to the form of Norwich's structural pillars. These, unlike Durham's thick and solid drums, are everywhere broken up by slender vertical columns, and throughout the cathedral floor-to-roof vaulting shafts (or "masts") also serve to carry the eye upwards. On the exterior, of course, Norwich's great needle-spire (315 feet high and built in the fifteenth century after lightning had brought down a predecessor) likewise points heavenwards, serving to balance the cathedral's unusually long nave.

Among the many splendid furnishings within the cathedral, special note should be taken of the bishop's throne (or *cathedra* in Latin, a cathedral being literally the church containing the prelate's seat) in the choir, parts of which date from the eighth century and come from Elmham, the original headquarters of the East Anglian diocese: and of the sculpture of a bishop on the north wall of the north transept. This may be the re-set tomb effigy of the cathedral-building Bishop Losinga, and if so it is the oldest surviving British example of such a memorial. Neither must the visitor miss Norwich's wonderful monastic cloisters, built between 1297 and 1430, with their unrivalled collection of some 400 figure-carved roof bosses.

See **Castles of the Norman Conquest.**

Norwich Cathedral's magnificent apsidal choir, its mightly pillars disguised and lightened by delicate clustering shafts.

OAKHAM CASTLE

Rutland, Leicestershire
OS 141 SK 863087

Oakham is twelve miles west of Stamford, and accessible from the A1 via the A606 westwards. The castle is in the town centre, set back from the road: and the fourteenth century parish church of All Saints is also worth a visit, as is the Rutland County Museum.

The great hall of Oakham Castle lies at the heart of the town, in quiet grounds which contrast with the busy traffic nearby. The hall, adorned with splendid figure sculpture, is one of the most beautiful and least spoilt of its kind. A hall at Oakham, belonging to William the Conqueror, is mentioned in the Domesday survey, but this refers to an earlier building, probably a substantial timber hall of possibly Saxon origin. William took over the prosperous manor of Oakham in 1075, on the death of Queen Edith, widow of King Edward the Confessor. Oakham was the central manor of the Rutland estates which were her dowry, and indeed had traditionally been part of the lands of the Saxon queens of England since the tenth century.

A motte and bailey castle was built, and slight remains of this motte can still be seen to the south-east of the present hall. The castle remained for many centuries the administrative and judicial centre of the royal manor, and of the Forest of Leicestershire and Rutland within which Oakham lay, as well as of the later shire of Rutland. The castle was never a typical feudal stronghold, but rather a fortified manor house. In the twelfth century it was granted to the Ferrers family,

and in about 1185 Wakelin de Ferrers built the present great hall of stone within the existing bailey. It is one of the finest examples of Norman domestic architecture in Europe, and the earliest British secular building with its decorative figure sculptures surviving, both inside and outside.

The roof outside has figures of Samson and of a centaur on the gables, and other figures on the walls. Inside, the body of the hall is open to the roof, with two arcades of stone columns separating it from the aisles. These and other parts of the hall are richly decorated with stone carvings of musicians, (animal and human) playing a variety of instruments, and carved heads and figures, some in an exciting naturalistic style. They and the intricate leaf carving on the column capitals can be traced by their unique character to the Kentish craftsmen who worked on the choir of Canterbury Cathedral. After the Canterbury choir was finished, these masons must have moved on up to the Midlands, where their work can also be seen at Grantham and Twyford. All round the hall walls hang decorative horseshoes, a toll which by tradition must be paid by every peer or monarch visiting Oakham for the first time.

By immemorial tradition, every monarch and peer who passes through Oakham must hang a symbolic horseshoe in its Norman castle hall.

The history of Old Sarum stretches back through the Saxon and Roman periods to the Iron Age, and the Normans were not slow to appreciate the strategic qualities of its location. They made use of the existing pre-Roman ramparts to protect the first town of Sarum, founded in the years c.1075–8. It was then that the first cathedral and the motte of the castle were built, but the confinement of a cathedral and a castle in the same small area led eventually to the founding of Salisbury: for, after interminable squabbling between priests and soldiers, the clergy moved down the hill to settle in the valley. The castle, a royal one since Stephen's time, remained within the great enclosure.

West of the gatehouse through the ramparts is the arrangement of buildings which served as the castle keep, surrounding an inner courtyard. All the masonry is now in ruins, but there was a chapel, a strong tower, and a hall, and the remains of these are clearly visible. The curtain wall also survives in stretches, and the whole gives a good impression of the strength of the position. Especially so when one climbs the ramparts to look down on the present city of Salisbury far below.

The headquarters of the Wessex diocese were moved here from Sherborne soon after the Conquest, and Bishop Osmund then built a cathedral in the north-west sector of the castle's outer bailey. This building, however, was destroyed soon after it was consecrated in 1092, and was replaced by another church in the early twelfth century. The foundations of both churches can be identified on the ground today.

OLD SARUM Wiltshire
OS 184 SU 138327
Old Sarum is two miles north of Salisbury city centre, off the A345 Salisbury-Amesbury road.

The massive foundations of the inner defensive walls. Below, the lofty access bridge to the motte.

Penhow is one of the most interesting castles in Wales, its well-preserved buildings admirably demonstrating the development from Norman stronghold to seventeenth century house. The castle has been the subject of careful archaeological investigation, which has greatly improved our understanding of its history. Originally the twelfth century defences, consisting of a bank and ditch, lay on the line of the present inner court. Within this there was a massive three-storied tower keep which, despite the insertion of a later twelfth century door, is essentially a Norman structure. Later in the twelfth century, a stone curtain wall was built to replace the earth rampart, and the first hall or public place was built against this. The earthworks of the bailey, extending south of the inner court, seem originally to have also protected the parish church.

PENHOW CASTLE Gwent
OS 171 ST 422908
The castle, a fascinating and surprising place to visit, stands near the A48, midway between Chepstow and Newport. From the M4, turn off at junction 22 (north end of the Severn Bridge) towards Chepstow, and then take the A48 towards Newport.

81

The twelfth century shrine and church of Pennant Melangell lie in a secluded valley below the beautiful Berwyn hills of northern Powys. St Melangell came here from Ireland in the eighth century to found a nunnery, whose boundaries are probably still represented by the typically Celtic circular churchyard. Her church, however, was rebuilt in the twelfth century: but within it are reminders of Melangell's most renowned legendary ex-

ploit, her miraculous preservation of a hare hunted by a local prince named Brochwel Ysgythrog, or "Brochwel with the tusks". Hares, therefore, peep from the folds of the dress worn by a fourteenth century effigy of the saint: while Melangell, Brochwel, the huntsman and the hare all appear in fragments of a late medieval wooden screen now used as a vestry partition. Originally, too, the beautiful twelfth century shrine which contained the saint's remains also stood in the church, but after fifteenth century alterations this was removed to a separate building called the *Cell-y-Bedd* ("room of the grave") which stands outside the eastern end of the present church, on the site of the original Roman-esque apse.

Though the re-set Norman south doorway of the church is also worthy of note, it is this shrine which is Pennant Melangell's principal treasure, a rare and remarkable survival unique in Britain and of European importance. Reconstructed from its scattered fragments in 1959, it is built of red sandstone, and consists of a coffin-sized relic chest with a steeply-pitched gabled roof, supported on columned arches. The arches and the heads of their columns are exuberantly carved with twisted and interlaced foliage and spirals, while the eastern gable of the relic chest is adorned with rows of lyre-shapes, also terminating in Celtic spirals. All the finely executed stone-carving, indeed, displays a distinctly Welsh spirit, and it was most probably the work of a team of local masons working under Norman influence.

PENNANT MELANGELL
Powys
OS 125 SJ 024265
This remote and secluded shrine is some fifteen miles south-east of Bala and the same distance north-west of Llanfyllin: it is reached from the Bala-Llanfyllin road (the B4391) by turning westwards in Llangynog, and following a signposted road for some two miles up the Tanat valley.

Opposite page, the unique Norman-Celtic shrine of Saint Melangell. Left, hares appear on this fourteenth-century effigy of Melangell, their Saintly protectress.

PEVENSEY CASTLE
East Sussex
OS 199 TQ 644048
The castle stands on Pevensey Level, on the A259 between Eastbourne and Hastings and thirteen miles west of the latter. In the picturesque little town, the medieval Mint House is worth a visit.

This Norman gateway pierces the massive Roman walls of Pevensey.

The Bayeux Tapestry depicts the Channel crossing by William's fleet of sailing ships. The inscription over the ships may be translated as "Here Duke William in a great ship crossed the sea and came to Pevensey", and the tapestry scenes then show the ships being beached and the horses and men disembarked. According to the contemporary chronicler William of Jumièges, William landed at Pevensey and built there a castle with a strong rampart, and from archaeological evidence we can assume that William saw the military value of the standing walls of the Roman fort at Pevensey, subsequently building his first English defences inside the Roman ramparts. The Norman defences were very simple at first, narrowing the former Roman west gate with a wall in front of the guard chambers and cutting away a curving ditch in front. The arch of the Roman east gate was also repaired, and fighting platforms were added to the top of the two towers further north. A pit containing a wooden ladder, cask, bowls and spades, with four eleventh century jugs from Normandy, has been excavated in the outer bailey.

Pevensey was granted to Robert Count of Mortain within a few years of the Conquest,

and he may have been responsible for the construction of the square inner bailey in the south-eastern corner of the fort, which was enclosed by a bank and ditch. Towards the end of the eleventh century a rectangular stone keep was built up against the Roman east wall inside the inner bailey.

The castle was starved into surrender by royal forces on two occasions: firstly in 1088, when it was held by Bishop Odo of Bayeux against William Rufus; and secondly in 1147, during the civil war between Stephen and Matilda. By the end of the thirteenth century the castle had fallen into disrepair, as the sea receded and Pevensey ceased to be a castle defending a coastline.

See **The Battle of Hastings.**

PORTCHESTER CASTLE
Hampshire
OS 196 SU 625046
Portchester is in the outer suburbs of Portsmouth, four miles north-west of the town centre via the A27 Portsmouth-Fareham road: the castle is on a promontory protruding into Portsmouth Harbour.

Like Pevensey, the Norman castle at Portchester occupies one corner of a Saxon Shore fort built during the Roman period, on a promontory in Portsmouth harbour. Portchester was a royal castle, founded by Henry I and built in about 1120, one of the most important fortifications on the south coast. Many kings of England, including Henry I himself, sailed from Portsmouth Harbour under the protection of this sternly solid structure.

The keep (square, squat and typically Norman) imposingly bestrides the north-west corner of the Roman circuit, protected on the outside by the Roman ditch. The keep was heightened by the addition of a third storey in about 1170. The bailey wall, with a later barbican or gateway, is also Norman; and is built in the same grey stone as the keep. Once inside, the compactness of the castle becomes most striking, for it is a wonderful embodiment of uncompromising Norman

84 *Henry I's fine Norman keep at Portchester, with the round-towered walls of the Roman fortress stretching away to the right.*

military ideals. Visitors may ascend the keep, the climb culminating in a spiral stairway. The effort is rewarded with a fine view of Portsmouth Harbour, the surrounding country, and of course the castle itself. It is from here that one best appreciates both Roman and medieval fortifications.

No visitor to Portchester should miss the church, which is in the south-east corner of the Roman fort. Once part of an Augustinian priory, founded in 1133, it is almost entirely Norman. Entrance is through the superb west front: and inside, the chancel and tower arches, nave pillars and font, all provide further excellent examples of Norman work. See **Pevensey Castle.**

Hidden deep in the rolling countryside of the Herefordshire/Shropshire border is the small, scattered village of Richard's Castle. It is now no more than a collection of pretty black and white cottages, dating mainly from the sixteenth and seventeenth centuries, but once it was Norman *Auretone*, mentioned in Domesday Book as the property of Osbern Fitz Richard. Some of the earthworks of the castle on the hill above the village may, however, be even earlier than this, for in 1052 the place was held by Richard son of Scrob, one of the Norman retainers of King Edward the Confessor. It is recorded that a number of these pioneering Norman lords built castles in England before the Conquest, and Richard's Castle is one of the strongest candidates for such a fortification. Apart from the twelfth century keep, most of the surviving masonry is thirteenth and fourteenth century, but the vast motte or mound is possibly part of a pre-Conquest construction. It is enclosed by a kidney-shaped bailey to the east, which has the remains of the original entrance in the south-east corner, and there seems to have been another enclosure on the west.

Immediately to the east of the castle, and originally protected by its outer bailey, is the church of St Bartholomew. This is an early Norman (i.e. post-1066) foundation, but the earliest surviving work is rather later than this and belongs to the twelfth century. The original church may have been cruciform in shape with a central tower, but now all that survives is the north wall of the nave, with its two round-headed windows, and the masonry at the east end of the chancel. The font too is probably twelfth century. The rest of the church was largely rebuilt during the fourteenth century, including the unusual detached bell tower.

In the fields to the north and east can be seen the traces of the bank and ditch which enclosed the nucleus of a small early medieval town. Inside are earthworks representing former property boundaries and buildings. For Richard's Castle is in fact a deserted Norman town, left high and dry as the area of conflict between the Anglo-Normans and the Welsh moved further westwards. See **Castles of the Norman Conquest.**

RICHARD'S CASTLE
Herefordshire
OS 137 SO 483703
The village is four miles south of Ludlow, on the B4361 back road to Leominster: the area is full of interest, and a few miles to the west are the great prehistoric hill-fort of Croft Ambrey and the National Trust's Croft Castle, a much-altered medieval fortress.

The lands which were to become the Honour of Richmond were granted by the Conqueror to one of his Breton folowers, Alan the Red (d.1084), probably in 1071 after the successful harrying of the north. Richmond was chosen as the centre of the new estates because of its defensive possibilities against both English and Danes, the potential enemies of its first Norman lord.

Built in the first generation after the Conquest, when normally castles were constructed of earth and timber, Richmond is unusual (particularly for a northern castle) as it was constructed from the outset in stone. In southern Britain both Colchester and the Tower of London were built of stone, but both were royal strongholds backed by all the resources that the crown could muster, while Richmond was built by a private individual.

The Norman site is triangular in plan, backing onto the cliffs overlooking the River Swale to the south. Building seems to have begun in the late 1080s, and to this period belong the curtain walls on the east and west sides, which incorporate herringbone masonry. The three towers of the east wall, at least at the ground-floor levels with their barrel-vaulting, also belong to the eleventh century.

Richmond Castle towers high above the River Swale.

RICHMOND CASTLE
North Yorkshire
OS 92 NZ 173007
The fine market town of Richmond is fifteen miles south-west of Darlington, and easily accessible from the nearby A1: the castle is in the town centre, in a most impressive position. To the west of Richmond is the splendid hill country of Swaledale.

The towering keep is a heightening of what was the original gatehouse, and the change in masonry between the original gatehouse and the upper storeys of the keep is clearly visible. Also note the delicate eleventh century column on the west side of the inner arch of the gatehouse.

Finally, in the south-east corner of the site, is another outstanding feature – Scolland's Hall, a rare example of an early Norman first floor hall. It is named after Scolland, lord of Bedale and steward to Alan, Earl of Brittany, though it was probably built in the time of Alan the Red (1071–89). The surviving stone staircase at the east end of the building, giving access from the basement to the first floor hall, is of particular interest.

Looking into the undercroft of Richmond's great tower-keep.

The interior of Scolland's Hall.

A group of Cistercians or "white monks" sent from Burgundy established the first Cistercian monastery in England at Waverley in Surrey in 1128, and another missionary group was sent out in 1131 to Yorkshire. This group was led by St Bernard of Clairvaux's own secretary, William, and it founded Rievaulx on the banks of the River Rye, on land given by Walter L'Espec, lord of Helmsley – who spent his last years in the abbey as a monk and was buried there in 1153.

From the Cistercian point of view, Rievaulx was a success as a missionary centre. Two of its abbots were canonised: the first abbot, William (1131–43) and the third abbot, Ailred (1147–67). It was so successful in attracting recruits that by the 1150s the house "... swarmed with monks like bees in a hive". The monastery also established daughter houses at Melrose and Warden in 1136, at Dundrennan in 1142 and at Revesby in 1143, as well as receiving the monks of Fountains into the order in 1133.

In the abbey church the transepts, the nave, and the western porch survive from the primary building of the 1130s. Most impressive are the round-headed and deeply-splayed windows of the transepts. Outside, the so-called library adjoining the south transept, and the east and west walls of the apsidal chapter house – with surviving stone seats and abbots' tombs – belong to the same period. Because of the spatial limitations of the site, the church is aligned north-south, so that what is conventionally called the south transept is strictly a west transept and hence

RIEVAULX ABBEY
North Yorkshire
OS 100 SE 577849

The abbey is some twenty-seven miles north of York and two and a half miles west of Helmsley (which has a fine castle): it can be reached from Helmsley either via the B1257 and a signposted minor road, or by a pleasant riverside walk.

is linked with the east wall of the chapter house. The lay brothers' range on the north side of the cloister, the infirmary cloister, and the buildings adjoining it also date from the late twelfth century: but the remainder of the majestic ruins, including the towering chancel, are principally the product of a major thirteenth century reconstruction. Remarkable both for its setting against a backdrop of wooded slopes and for its well-preserved buildings, Rievaulx amply repays a visit.

87

Norman Architecture

Norman architecture is one of the best known and most instantly recognisable English architectural styles. Its roots, however, lie not in Britain but on the continent, and derive ultimately from Roman classical architecture. Indeed in western Europe (where the style is called Roman or Romanesque) there are a number of buildings dating back to the Roman period which bear many of the hallmarks of what we in Britain have come to call "Norman" architecture.

The extent to which Anglo-Saxon architecture was part of an insular and backward tradition has been hotly debated by scholars. It is true that many of the great Anglo-Saxon churches (like Bradford-upon-Avon, Brixworth and Earls Barton) display the use of the round arch and other significant elements of "Norman" architecture, but they cannot truly be called Romanesque. Indeed the great majority of Saxon churches were built of wood, although only one such, the tiny church of Greensted – juxta – Ongar in Essex, survives today.

However, the commonly held belief that "Norman" architecture did not appear in England until after the Conquest of 1066 is equally mistaken. Signs of the new style first began to emerge during the reign of the penultimate Saxon king, Edward the Confessor (1042–1066). His Westminster Abbey, completed just before his death, had close affinities with many buildings in Normandy, including the great abbey at Jumièges on the Seine and the church of the abbey on Mont St Michel.

On a much smaller scale too, it is often difficult to distinguish between Anglo-Saxon and Norman work in the parish churches of the late eleventh century. This is the period called by scholars the Saxo-Norman overlap; namely the time when English masons, still deeply aware of their own skills and traditions, were working in a new and unfamiliar style, to the orders of their new Norman masters. Thus in some instances both Anglo-Saxon and Norman motifs, often of the same date and perhaps even by the same hand, can be found side by side in the same church.

But if the Normans were not solely responsible for the introduction of the Romanesque style into Britain, they certainly were responsible for its widespread adoption within only a few years of the Conquest. The introduction of their architectural style, indeed, appears to have been one of the ways in which the Normans impressed their will on the English people. Few buildings can be more intimidating than the White Tower at the Tower of London. Begun in the 1070s, and as its name implies originally brilliantly whitewashed, it stood guard over the city as a symbol of Norman power and authority. The massive keep at Colchester and the slightly later one at Norwich must have had a similar impact on these towns' inhabitants. In church architecture too, the Normans favoured the strong and massive. In many respects the new cathedrals like Durham, St Albans and, perhaps most of all, Winchester must have looked like fortresses. Certainly they were in stark contrast to anything that had gone before.

What then are the principal characteristics of Norman architecture? Although it is true that the use of the round arch was not new in Britain, the adoption of the massive semi-circular and sometimes (as at Durham and Selby) decorated arch undoubtedly was. The idea of terminating the east end of a church with a semi-circular "apse" instead of a straight wall was another important Norman innovation, though admittedly there are a few examples of this feature in pre-Conquest churches. Nearly all the large abbeys and cathedrals rebuilt by the Normans before 1100 terminated in apsidal east ends and chapels, but unfortunately very few of these now survive. In parish churches too, early Norman chancels took the form of apses (especially in the south-east where contacts with France were strongest) and fine examples can still be seen in many places.

The storied composition of wall-elevations was another characteristic of Norman design. The interior walls of Saxon churches, although often lofty, were rarely of more than one level, but the Normans introduced galleries and clerestories – second and third tiers of arches rising above the main line of arches on the lowest storey of the wall: and many of these three-tiered features survive today, as at Romsey Abbey, Peterborough and Norwich cathedrals, and a number of the larger parish churches.

In ornamentation, the most familiar Norman motif is probably the chevron (zig-zag or dogtooth) pattern, while the use of "beak heads" – crow-like heads with prominent beaks – was common in the decoration of their arches. Another much favoured design was the use of intersecting arches carved in low relief, still seen to such good effect on the west fronts of Lincoln and Rochester cathedrals or on the elaborate forebuilding at Castle Rising. Grotesque figures, exemplified at Kilpeck (Herefordshire), also feature heavily in the embellishment of doorways and the lines of corbels beneath roof-eaves, while much of the best Norman sculpture is to be found in the tympana (a tympanum being the semi-circular space between the top of a door and the round-headed arch above) of parish churches up and down the country. Barfreston (Kent) and Stretton Sugwas (Herefordshire) are two of the best examples.

Developments in military architecture were on the whole slower, and perhaps the most significant change was in the choice of building materials. The majority of the immediately post-Conquest castles (with one or two notable exceptions like the White Tower in London and Colchester) were of earth and timber construction, but during the twelfth century many were rebuilt in stone. This process can be well illlustrated at a number of individual sites, two of the best examples being at Farnham (Surrey) and Rochester. In the second half of the century, a particular feature was the emergence of spectacular and experimental round or polygonal tower keeps like Conisborough (Yorkshire), Orford (Suffolk) and Pembroke (Dyfed).

In this brief survey most of the emphasis has been on ecclesiastical architecture, and in particular on the greater churches. This is partly because, apart from some of the great Norman castles like Portchester, Richmond and Dover, it is the churches which have survived best; and also because it was primarily through church architecture that the Norman style developed and spread.

Survivals of Norman domestic buildings are much rarer. This is probably because many were of wood and, of course, a large number were replaced in the later Middle Ages. Of those that do remain, the houses in Lincoln and Southampton are among the best urban examples, while in the countryside the first floor hall at Boothby Pagnell is a classic of the type.

*Rochester is thirty miles south-east of
London, via the A2: the castle and
cathedral stand together in a
prominent position by the Medway,
and can also be fleetingly glimpsed by
travellers crossing the M2 Medway
Bridge.*

In Norman England cathedral and castle often stood adjacent to each other as a clear representation of the interdependence of secular and church power: and nowhere is this relationship better expressed than at Rochester on the Medway estuary. Ecclesiastically and architecturally Rochester cathedral is somewhat overshadowed by its neighbour at Canterbury, but nonetheless it is an extremely impressive building. Rochester, together with London, was one of the two sees founded by St Augustine in 604, just seven years after he established his church at Canterbury. But by the time of the Norman Conquest the cathedral, which had witnessed much strife and turmoil during the later Saxon period, was apparently "almost falling to pieces with age".

In 1077, however, the energetic reformer Gundulf – who also designed the Tower of London – was appointed bishop of Rochester, and he set about building an entirely new Norman cathedral, which was also to be the church of a major Benedictine monastery. Of this cathedral, the principal remains are the western part of the underground crypt and the square "Gundulf's Tower", now enveloped by the north transept but originally intended to be free-standing and perhaps designed for defence. The rest of the church was rebuilt in the mid twelfth century after a fire, and from this second Norman reconstruction survive part of the nave and, most impressively, the twin-towered west front, with its magnificent and ornately sculpted central doorway, surmounted by a figure of Christ in Majesty.

To defend the strategic crossing of the River Medway, Gundulf also built a stone castle at Rochester: but only fragments of this

remain, and the great tower keep which still dominates the city is the work of William of Corbeil, Archbishop of Canterbury. Begun in 1127, it is the tallest keep in Britain, standing 125 feet high and seventy feet square, with walls twelve feet thick. Within are four storeys of rooms (all now unfloored) and the interior of the whole building is divided into two halves by a massive ground-to-roof cross wall, designed both to add structural strength and to allow defenders to hold out in one half of the keep even after the other had fallen. This was put to the test during the great siege of 1215, when King John's attackers undermined the southern corner tower and burst in, but were for a time unable to dislodge the stubborn garrison from behind their cross wall.

Left, the richly decorated west door of Rochester Cathedral. Top, behind this mighty cross-wall in Rochester Castle keep, the garrison held out against King John's assault in 1215. Above, Bishop Gundulf's crypt beneath the cathedral choir.

91

ROMSEY ABBEY

Hampshire OS 185 SU 351213

Romsey is ten miles north of Southampton, on the A3057; east of the market place is a thirteenth century house called King John's Hunting Box.

Founded in 907, the wealthy nunnery at Romsey had considerable holdings at the time of Domesday, which included property in Winchester and a number of rural manors: it was also much favoured by royal princesses. In 1086 Christine, the sister of the Saxon prince Edgar the Atheling, became abbess: and her young niece, Maud, stayed there for a while before becoming Henry I's queen in 1100. King Stephen's daughter Mary became abbess in 1160, and it was probably her uncle,

Bishop Henry of Blois, who was responsible for much of the architecture we see today.

The church, cruciform in plan and 256 feet long, is built of Chilmark stone from quarries near Salisbury. The present magnificent building dates, in its earliest parts, from the 1120s. Of this period are the tower, the transepts, with their interesting semi-circular chapels, and the chancel. Externally the church is impressively Norman: while internally the building is spacious and imposing,

Opposite, three views of Norman arches – arcade, gallery and clerestory – in the chancel of Romsey Abbey. Left, these distinctive nave pillars, linking the first and second tiers, are a Romsey speciality much initiated elsewhere. Below, a view down the side aisle.

and it is also architecturally very complex. In the chancel aisles there are some superb figurative capitals, while in the chancel itself rise three tiers of arches, the arcade, gallery, and clerestory. The nave starts with two bays which have a massive round pillar running from the arcade through to the gallery. This feature can also be seen at Gloucester, Tewkesbury, and as far away as Jedburgh: but at Romsey this design appears to have been soon abandoned, as the other pillars in the nave are different in form. This section of the nave would appear to date from the latter half of the twelfth century, while the last three bays to the west are of early thirteenth century date and are Early English in style. At the Dissolution of the Monasteries in 1538 the church was bought by the town and that saved it from demolition. All the other monastic buildings were destroyed.

See **Jedburgh Abbey.**

Henry of Blois' Norman nave at Romsey Abbey, with its remarkable double-arched gallery.

ST ALBANS CATHEDRAL
Hertfordshire
OS 166 TL 145071
The picturesque town of St Albans is about twenty miles north of London, via either the M1 (exit 7) or the A1 and the A6: the traveller should also visit the extensive remains of Roman Verulamium nearby, and perhaps patronise the Fighting Cocks, said to be the oldest inn in England.

As early as A.D. 400, a shrine and church had been established on the hilltop site of the execution of the early third century Romano-British martyr, St Alban. This was re-endowed by King Offa of Mercia in about 793, and by the time of the Norman Conquest St Albans was one of the wealthiest Benedictine abbeys in England.

All, however, was swept away during the abbacy of Paul of Caen (1077–93), nephew of Lanfranc, the first Norman Archbishop of Canterbury. Doubtless motivated partly by a desire to outdo his uncle's work at Canterbury and partly by a wish to reform what he considered a corrupt and backward community, Paul embarked, with considerable determination and single-mindedness, on a comprehensive rebuilding programme. Remarkably, this was to be accomplished within eleven years of his taking office.

When complete the new church was 360 feet in length, with a nave of ten bays, crossing tower and transepts, and an apsidal choir flanked by shorter apsidal chapels, with further semi-circular apses on the east sides of the transepts. Much of this still survives, notably the nine round-headed arches on the north side of the nave and the four Norman arches on the south, the massive crossing arches and the monumental transepts. Pride of place must go, however, to the central tower. Constructed almost entirely of brick taken from the nearby Roman city of *Verulamium* and rising to a height of 144 feet, it still dominates the town and surrounding countryside.

In time Paul's church itself began to look old-fashioned, and just over a hundred years later much of it was re-built in the new Early English style by Abbot John of Cella. He was responsible for lengthening the nave, making it the longest in Europe at 285 feet (a distinction it still holds) but his ambitious plans for rebuilding the west front had to be dropped owing to lack of money in 1197. The present west front, indeed, was not built until 1879, two years after the great abbey church was raised to the status of a cathedral.

The red sandstone priory lies at the mouth of a narrow gorge, where the Pow Beck runs out towards the sea, now over half a mile away. It is overlooked by the village on the other side of the stream. The priory is thought to have been built on the site of a nunnery founded in *c*.650 by St Bega (or St Bee) from Ireland.

In 1120 William le Meschin, lord of Egremont, founded a Benedictine house here for a prior and six monks, sent out from St Mary's Abbey at York. The house remained small and was dissolved by Henry VIII in 1539.

Although the domestic buildings have long since gone, some Norman work survives intact in the present church. The oldest surviving part is the magnificent weatherbeaten west doorway, dating from *c*.1150, which has elaborate sculptured decoration on the arch. Inside, the north transept is thought to date from *c*.1150, and the chancel, crossing arches and nave arcade are Early English of *c*.1200. An interesting twelfth century grave slab with a sword, a bowman, and a pair of stirrups between four horseshoes is now on display with a number of other grave slabs and a Saxon cross. Outside, opposite the west door, is a well preserved stone pediment lintel of *c*.1120, with a carving of St Michael and the dragon surrounded by Scandinavian-style tracery. Below this is a small round-headed cross of a similar period.

In 1981 archaeologists excavating an aisle adjoining the chancel discovered a lead wrapped, clay packed burial containing the extraordinarily well-preserved body of a man. "St Bees Man" was buried between 1300 and 1500, and is of particular interest to archaeologists, historians and doctors, since very few bodies of this period have been found in a comparable state in England.

ST BEES PRIORY Cumbria
OS 89 NX 968122
St Bees is on the Cumbrian coast and the B5345, five miles south of Whitehaven : immediately adjacent to the church is the Elizabethan St Bees school, and three miles east is Egremont, with the ruins of a Norman castle.

The Tironensian abbey of St Mary the Virgin was founded here in 1115, to the south of an existing parish church. However, finds of Celtic sculpture suggest that a Christian monastic community had existed here since the sixth century, and, as so often in Wales, the establishment of Norman monks represented an act of political as well as spiritual policy, acting as a counterweight to the Celtic Christianity which provided a haven for anti-Norman sentiment and resistance.

Although the greater part of the church and cloister are ruined, something of the plan of the twelfth century church can be deciphered. It was a cruciform church with a central transeptal crossing, a very large choir and no aisles. Over the last thirty years, the site has been in the care of the Historic Buildings and Monuments authority for Wales, and the surrounding stonework and foundations have been conserved and displayed. This work enables the chronology of changing building alignments to be seen clearly, as each generation of monks adapted the original abbey plan to their own needs.

The ruins of St Dogmael's Abbey church, seen from the site of the chapter house.

ST DOGMAEL'S ABBEY
Dyfed
OS 145 SN 164458
The abbey is on the west Wales coast and the Teifi estuary, a mile west of Cardigan via the B4546.

95

SCARBOROUGH CASTLE

North Yorkshire
OS 101 TA 048892

*The castle dominates the famous
seaside resort of Scarborough, which
is forty miles north-east of York via the
A64.*

The castle occupies a headland to the north and east of Scarborough, a site which has attracted settlement since prehistoric times. On the eastern edge of the site the ditch and bank of a fourth century Roman signal station now enclose the foundations of the successive medieval chapels of the castle. The castle dominates the town. Everything about it is impressive – its massive moat, its barbican gate, the stone bridge, its curtain wall, and above all, its keep.

The castle was clearly built for action, as a major centre in the defence of the north-east. Even its military record is impressive, since although many times besieged, it has never fallen by assault alone. A garrison was maintained here until the nineteenth century and the castle last saw military action in December 1914, when it was bombarded by ships of the Imperial German Navy.

Parts of the castle complex date back to the 1130s, when William le Gros, Earl of Yorkshire, built it as his principal residence.

The curtain wall defending the landward side of the headland, but not the wall towers, belongs to the first period of building. Originally, the wall followed the line of the scarp overlooking the stone bridge, and it is probable that the original gatehouse stood on the site of the present keep.

The keep can be dated from documentary evidence to 1158–69. Built to the orders of Henry II, this massive, four-storeyed structure is one of the finest of its kind in the land. It is fifty-six feet square and survives to a height of eighty-five feet. The hall is on the first floor, and it was at this level that the building was entered, by way of a flight of covered stone steps on its south face.

The second of the three chapels on the site of the Roman signal station is also of Norman date, as demonstrated by its carved decorations. Finally, the foundations of a large twelfth century building of unknown function may be seen immediately to the south-east of the bailey ditch.

*Above, the vital well in the castle
courtyard. Right, despite deliberate
"slighting" after the Civil War, much
of Scarborough's keep still stands,
testifying to the strength of Norman
mortar and masonry.*

Dominating the east end of the market place, this fine church is all that remains of the great Benedictine abbey of St Mary and St Germane. The abbey owes its foundation to Benedict, a monk of Auxerre who established himself as a hermit in the Selby area in 1068. His reputation as a holy man and miracle-worker spread, and so impressed the Sheriff of York that he introduced Benedict to the king, then on his northern campaigns. The Conqueror granted lands to Benedict to build an abbey, which thus became the earliest major Benedictine monastery to be founded in northern England. The abbey church ceased to be monastic in 1539 and became parochial in 1618.

The surviving Norman structures are all in the west part of the church, in the nave and north transept. Of particular note on the outside are the fine west door, the flat buttresses and the corbel table of the south aisle, the window in the west wall of the north transept, and the lower courses of the central tower. Internally, the massed round nave pillars are impressive, particularly "Hugh's pillar" on the south side of the nave: this is named after Abbot Hugh de Lacy (1097–1123) who began work on the Norman church as we see it today.

SELBY ABBEY
North Yorkshire
OS 105 SE 615324
The market town and port of Selby is twelve miles south of York on the A19; a mile south, on the A19, is the parish church of Brayton, with its Norman tower, fine doorway, and carvings within.

Top, a cluster of shafts supporting the nave gallery arch, apparently an experimental feature at Selby Abbey. Above, Trelliswork decoration on "Hugh's pillar". On page 98, the late Norman west portal of the abbey.

The only upstanding remnant of the medieval settlement at Sempringham is the parish church of St Andrew, which stands alone amid the fields and the earthworks of the substantial priory which was the mother-house of the order of Gilbertine canons, the only monastic order wholly English in origin. The order was founded by St Gilbert, a local priest, during the 1130s, and consisted primarily of a community of nuns with an associated institute of regular canons. Sempringham was a double house – that is it consisted of two complete sets of conventual buildings, one for the women and one for the men, separated by the church in which both groups worshipped. The church itself was divided by a central division in such a way that both groups could see the high altar: but has now completely disappeared.

The surviving Norman parish church, which was distinct from that of the priory, has been much altered, and only a portion of the original cruciform plan remains. However, the south doorway is a notable original feature, complete with its fir wood doors decorated with Norman iron scroll work.

SEMPRINGHAM CHURCH
Lincolnshire
OS 130 TF 107329
The "lost village" of Sempringham is eight miles north of Bourne, in the fields north-west of Pointon. From Bourne, take the A15 north, turning off onto the B1177 through Dunsby, Dowsby and Pointon. Half a mile north of Pointon, opposite a road turning east to Sempringham House Farm, is the track leading west to the church.

Though much altered, the lonely church at Sempringham preserves its Norman nave. The church is usually kept locked but the key is available from the vicar in the village of Billingborough close by.

Despite strong Norman associations, Shrewsbury possesses relatively little surviving Norman architecture. By the time of the Norman Conquest the town had five churches, and between 1067 and 1069 Roger de Montgomery built a castle here consisting of an oval motte, an inner bailey, and an outer bailey of uncertain extent. This was thrown up at the neck of a loop of the Severn, so that only 300 yards remain to be guarded. The Domesday Book recorded that fifty-one houses were destroyed when Shrewsbury Castle was built. In 1069 "the Welsh, with the men of Cheshire, laid siege to the King's castle at Shrewsbury, aided by the townsmen under Edric the Wild", and during the next century the castle was rebuilt in stone by Henry II. Only the round-arched gateway can claim to be genuinely Norman, since elsewhere in the fortress there has been repeated rebuilding and renovation. But it is the site of the castle, dominating the skyline of the town still, that reminds us of the Norman skill in choosing the best strategic sites and manipulating them for administrative and commercial advantage.

Elsewhere in the town, on the southern side of the English Bridge, Roger de Montgomery built a Benedictine monastery – Shrewsbury Abbey. In 1094 Roger entered his own foundation as a monk and died there three days later: according to the historian Ordericus Vitalis (who was born just five miles away at Atcham) Roger was buried in the new church between the two altars. It is possible, therefore, that much of the interior of the abbey church we see today can be dated to the late eleventh century. Certainly there is much forceful plain building of a military type here that would indicate such an early date.

SHREWSBURY Shropshire
OS 126 SJ 495128
Shrewsbury is 150 miles north-west of London via the M1, M6, M54 and A5. The castle is in the town centre, by the railway station, and the abbey church (Holy Cross) is to the south on the Abbey Foregate, near the A49 and the by-pass. St Mary's church (St Mary's Place) is notable for its spire, its Norman work within, and its collection of stained glass; and there are many fine Tudor houses in the town.

SKIPSEA BROUGH
Humberside
OS 107 TA 162551
*Skipsea is on the Yorkshire coast,
eight miles south of Bridlington via
the A165 and the B1242: the castle
stands near the road, desolate but
most impressive.*

Skipsea was founded in 1086, when Drogo
de Bevrière built an unusual motte and bailey
castle here. He also attempted, unsuccessfully, to establish a port and market town at
the castle gate.

The motte is forty-six feet high, and is built
on an island in a former lake. It is connected
to a bailey, 100 yards away on the lake bank,
by a causeway. The motte is further fortified
by an outer ditch and bank. The bailey covers

eight and a half acres on a nearby ridge. The
three sides away from the lake are defended
by a ditch and bank, and on the east, the
natural slope down to the mere has been artificially steepened. Today the lake is a bog,
and Skipsea Brough is only a hamlet. A fragment of stone walling running down the side
of the mound is all that remains of the castle
buildings themselves.

SOUTHAMPTON Hampshire
OS 196 SU 423110
*Southampton is seventy-seven miles
south-west of London, via the M3 and
A33. It has a most impressive set of
medieval town defences, sections of
which can be seen near both King
John's House and Canute's Palace,
while a fine stretch runs the length of
Western Esplanade. The Bargate, in
Bargate Street nearby, incorporates a
medieval guildhall.*

*The gable end of Canute's Palace is
well preserved. Below, this fireplace
once heated a first-floor Solar, a
private chamber.*

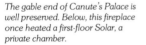

Southampton does not give the immediate
impression of being an historic town. However, it is well endowed with a range of Norman buildings, several of which were revealed
by bomb damage during the Second World
War. Most notable among these are two mer-
chants' houses, the so-called King John's
House and Canute's Palace.

King John's House is situated in the garden of Tudor House Museum, Bugle Street.
The best features are, internally, the first floor
windows in the west wall and the fireplace in
the north wall. Externally a blocked round-
headed arch is visible at ground level on the
west side. The building dates from c.1160.

Canute's Palace can be found on Porters
Lane at the south end of the High Street. Like
King John's House, this is a first floor hall
house of the 1160–70s: but whereas King
John's House is rectangular, Canute's Palace
is long and narrow. The most interesting features are in the south wall, including the
remains of a double doorway at first floor

level. The west wall is a recent rebuild, but
uses old materials, including a characteristic
Norman window.

Contrasting with these domestic buildings
are the remains at the castle. The Norman
work is marked by six buttresses, and the western facade has a round-headed and single-
light window, both modern rebuilds. The
doorway gives access to the Castle Vault, a
rectangular tunnel-vaulted chamber. To the
south of this building are the remains of the
Castle Hall, a first floor hall house which has
been much altered. The twenty-four joist
holes, newel staircase, and the remains of two
blocked windows in the west wall are of particular interest, and there is a deep garderobe
(or lavatory) in the external south-east corner.
Elsewhere in the town, St. Michael's church
(though very much altered) has at its core the
base of an early Norman tower. It also contains a Norman black Tournai marble font.
See **Lincoln.**

100

The collegiate church of Southwell was one of four foundations for secular canons in the medieval diocese of York, the others being at York, Ripon and Beverley. The church was raised to cathedral status in 1884.

Its early history is obscure. Ealdred, archbishop of York (1061–69) seems to have acquired the manor of Southwell in about 1066, and the foundation of the collegiate church probably followed soon after. The earliest surviving buildings, however, date from c.1108.

The Norman portions of this small cathedral are confined to the transepts, central tower, the nave, and the west front. On the exterior the tower and the north transept with its round-headed windows are particularly worthy of note. So, too, is the west front which preserves much of its original Norman appearance, being plain and flat with pyramidal roofs (rebuilt 1880) on the two west towers. The large west window is an addition of the fifteenth century. The nave has massive round pillars supporting a gallery and clerestory, and the clerestory windows are rounded on the exterior – an unusual design. The rest of the church belongs to the thirteenth and fourteenth centuries, for the Norman east end was replaced in the 1230s and the octagonal chapter-house, perhaps the glory of the building, was added in c.1300.

SOUTHWELL MINSTER
Nottinghamshire
OS 120 SK 702538
Southwell is six miles west of Newark and the A1 and sixteen miles north-east of Nottingham, via the A612.

STAMFORD BRIDGE
Humberside
OS 106 SE 712556
The village is nine miles east of York, on the A166 road to Bridlington.

Near this weir, in 1066, the English fought their way across the Derwent to defeat the Scandinavian invaders at the battle of Stamford Bridge.

At Stamford Bridge, on the 25th of September 1066, King Harold of England completely defeated the Norwegian army led by their King Harald Hardrada, before marching south to fight William of Normandy at Hastings. There had been an important river crossing here since at least Roman times. A natural ford across the River Derwent is provided by a sandstone outcrop, and Roman roads approach from four directions. By 1066 a narrow wooden bridge had been built, probably a few yards downstream from the ford. Hardrada was encamped on both sides of the river when the English approached unexpectedly from the west. Despite a Norwegian attempt to hold the bridge, the English fought their way across and the final struggle took place south-east of the village, at a place still called Battle Flats.

Today Stamford Bridge is a pleasant place to visit and picnic. A weir marks the location of the original ford, and a watermill probably occupies the site of one mentioned in Domesday Book.

STRATA FLORIDA Dyfed
OS 135 SN 746658

The abbey ruins stand on the edge of the wild country of the Cambrian Mountains, some twenty miles south-east of Aberystwyth : they are reached via a signposted minor road turning west in Pontrhydfendigaid, on the B4343 Aberystwyth-Tregaron road. The abbey museum is worth a visit, and nearby is the tomb of the famous Welsh poet Dafydd ap Gwilym : note also the curious "grave of a leg" by the modern church's door.

Set deep in the lovely and remote countryside so beloved of the Cistercian order, Strata Florida ("flowery vale") was nevertheless once situated on an important trade and pilgrimage route. Today the main road lies several miles to the north, but in the Middle Ages it ran close to the abbey, enabling the monks to display to amazed travellers an ancient wooden bowl which they claimed was the "Holy Grail".

The abbey was founded in 1164 (on a site about two miles to the south-west of the present ruins) by the Anglo-Norman baron,

outwardly of standard Cistercian type with an aisled nave, north and south transepts (each with three eastern chapels) and a square-ended presbytery. It formerly had a central tower, and the domestic buildings lay around a cloister to the south. The nave arcades are, however, unique, for they consist of pillars set on top of screen walls, which completely block off the aisles from the central part of the nave, this being reserved as the lay brothers' place of worship. It was perfectly usual for the church in a Cistercian house to be divided into separate parts for the monks

The original floor tiles still survive in this ruined chapel at Strata Florida.

Robert Fitz Stephen. Soon after, however, his estates were captured by the Welsh lord, Rhys ap Gruffydd, and the abbey passed into Welsh patronage. In 1184 the monks moved to the present site, which became a centre of Welsh culture and literature, and it was here that the country's annals (*Brut y Tywysogion*) were written. Despite the destruction caused during the Welsh rebellion against Edward I in 1294 and by the revolt of Owen Glyndwr in the early fifteenth century, the abbey was one of the richest in Wales, with its wealth based chiefly on wool production. By the end of the middle ages, this prosperity had declined, and by the Dissolution in 1539 there were only seven monks left.

Although somewhat fragmentary, the ruins are of considerable interest. The church, which was built in the late twelfth or early thirteenth century in a transitional style, is

and lay brethren, but the arrangement at Strata Florida is not found anywhere else in England or Wales.

The closest parallels are in Ireland, and this may also have been the inspiration for the unusual west doorway, the most impressive relic now on the site. This is round-headed, and framed by five continuous mouldings which are cut at regular intervals by unbroken banding, each band ending in a spiral-like decoration outside the main framework of the door.

Also worth seeing are the fine glazed floor tiles re-set in the transeptal chapels (where they are protected by modern timber roofs). These tiles formerly floored the whole of the east end, local slates being used in the rest of the church. Less survives of the monastic buildings, and the site of the refectory and kitchen is covered by the present farmhouse.

At first sight the church of Mary Magdalen at Stretton Sugwas seems an unlikely destination for the visitor in search of Norman Britain. It is essentially a Victorian church, but inside there is a remarkable surprise, a re-set Norman typanum showing Samson struggling with a lion, sitting astride the animal and forcing open its jaws. It has been argued that this image, locally executed by a sculptor of the Hereford School, was based on an original at Parthenay-le-Vieux in the Poitou region of western France. The French church lies on the pilgrimage route to Santiago de Compostela, whose churches were to inspire so much twelfth century Romanesque architecture. But whatever its origins, this remarkable twelfth century gem should not be missed.

STRETTON SUGWAS
Herefordshire
OS 149 SO 464425
Stretton Sugwas is three miles north-west of Hereford city centre, just off the A438 Hereford-Kington road.

TEWKESBURY ABBEY
Gloucestershire
OS 150 SO 890324
Tewkesbury is eight miles north-west of Cheltenham, and a mile from junction 9 of the M5: it contains a wealth of splendid house, predominantly of the seventeenth and eighteenth centuries.

Massive round pillars between the nave and south aisle of Tewkesbury Abbey.

Originally the church of a Benedictine monastery, founded in 1102 by Robert Hamon, Tewkesbury Abbey is today one of the finest Norman parish churches in England. During the Middle Ages the west end of the nave served as the town's parish church, and this saved the whole church from demolition at the time of the Dissolution. The town bought the church from Henry VIII in 1542 for £452, which represented the value of its bells and the lead from its roofs and windows.

A large part of the church is twelfth century and built of local stone, with some rebuilding, mainly in the fourteenth century. The most notably Norman feature outside is the tower – a landmark in the district. On the lower storey of each side it is possible to see the outline of the original steeply pitched wooden roofs of the church. The north wall of the nave still has its decorative arcading (now pierced by later windows) and great north porch. The west front was originally more impressive, with the steeply pitched Norman roof showing above the soaring arches.

Entering the abbey through the north door there is a great feeling of space, for this is one of the largest parish churches in England and is bigger than some cathedrals. The nave has the characteristic massive round pillars and semi-circular arches, but the roof was lowered in the fourteenth century and the vaulted ceiling inserted. At the same time a ceiling was put in at the base of the tower, which was originally open; the Norman decoration above can thus only be appreciated from the top of the tower. The south transept still retains one of the original semi-circular chapels – the Lady Chapel – but a mosaic now fills the Norman window. Next to this chapel is the night stair which gave access to the church from the monks' dormitory. Notable among Tewkesbury Abbey's post-Norman features are its splendid monuments and memorial chapels, especially the Despenser Chantry with its effigy of a kneeling knight.

TICKENCOTE CHURCH
Leicestershire
OS 141 SK 980095

Tickencote is three miles north-west of historic Stamford, immediately south of the A1.

The small stone-built village of Tickencote lies in the peaceful valley of the Gwash, just south of the busy Great North Road, the Roman Ermine Street. Its tiny church, hidden away here, provides startling riches for the visitor, with its sumptuous and somewhat puzzling late Norman workmanship.

The east end of the exterior was restored in 1792 and is richly ornamented with arcading, buttresses, windows, recesses and carved corbel heads over the entire height of the gable wall. Inside, the rib vault of the chancel roof is unique in English parish churches, and is the earliest example in England, even earlier than that in Canterbury Cathedral. At the centre of the vault is a rare boss, carved

with three heads, a monk and two muzzled bears, and there is a priest's chamber in the roof space above.

The most extraordinary feature of the church, however, is the large and fantastically decorated (if carelessly constructed) chancel arch, which has now spread and settled to an irregular half eclipse. On the nave side are six elaborately moulded and enriched bands of decoration with two more towards the chancel. Each is carved with different designs, including a row of grotesque animal and human heads of great variety, and the arch is remarkable for its size, elaboration and curious details. These include a 'Green Man' and a variety of fantastical animals.

TOTNES Devon
OS 202 SX 800605

Totnes is in south Devon, six miles west of Paignton and twenty-two miles south-west of Exeter via the A38 and A385. The fifteenth century church of St Mary, with its splendid tower, is also worth a visit: as is the town's Guildhall, once part of Totnes Priory.

Totnes stands on a hill rising from the west bank of the River Dart. Founded in Anglo-Saxon times as a royal *burh* or fortified town, it was granted soon after the Conquest to Judhael, a Breton soldier in Norman service who became one of the greatest landowners in the West Country. He, it appears, founded the castle, which like so many other early Norman strongholds took the form of a steep-sided motte and an attached bailey, both of which are still clearly apparent. The earth for the motte was thrown up round a central core of unmortared stones, whose outline is marked out, and which was intended to form a solid base for the fifteen foot square wooden tower which originally topped the mound.

But subsequently, probably during the twelfth century, this fire-vulnerable building was replaced by the stone "shell-keep" whose wall (strengthened later in the middle ages) still rings the motte top: such shell keeps seem to have been a particularly popular form of late Norman fortification here in the west, where comparable examples also still survive at Launceston, Restormel and Trematon in Cornwall.

The town walls of Totnes, parts of which can still be seen, may also be of late Norman date: their round-arched north gate stands near the castle; while the eastern gate, much rebuilt, picturesquely bridges the High Street.

TRETOWER Powys
OS 161 SO 184212

The castle and manor house are nine miles north-west of Abergavenny, on the A40/A479 road from Abergavenny to Talgarth. The similar round tower at Bronllys is a mile north-west of Talgarth (at SO 149346).

The original entrance to the great round keep at Tretower, beneath the V-shaped gable, was raised well above ground level, and the wall of the earlier keep was used as an outer defence.

Picturesquely set in the Usk valley, against the backdrop of the Black Mountains and the Brecon Beacons, the remarkable series of buildings at Tretower demonstrate with unique clarity the development of a medieval castle. Its history begins in the late eleventh century, when the Norman freebooter Ber-

nard of Neufmarché seized the lordship of Brecon from the Welsh and distributed its lands among his followers. The Tretower region fell to one Picard, who built there the motte and bailey castle whose ditches and earthworks, originally defended by wooden stockades, can still be discerned. Then, a generation later, Picard's son Roger replaced the wooden defences of the motte by a gate-housed stone wall, within which was an L-shaped block containing a hall, a solar or private chamber, and a kitchen. But this fortress (which still stands to almost its full height in places) apparently did not suit his descendants: and in about 1240 Roger's great-grandson, another Roger, decided to build a great round-tower keep of the type then very fashionable in the Welsh borders – there being another example, for instance, some ten miles to the north, at Bronllys near Talgarth. Instead of entirely removing his great-grandfather's castle, however, Roger simply demolished its interior walls and raised his new keep inside, blocking up the doors and windows of the earlier building and using its shell as part of the outer defences round his new stronghold.

Roger's economically composite fortress, nevertheless, enjoyed only a short period of use: for by about 1300 it had been abandoned in favour, not of a new castle proper, but of a more comfortable fortified manor house called Tretower Court, on a new site 200 yards to the south-east. Much rebuilt during the fifteenth century, Tretower Court survives virtually complete, one of the finest of its kind in Britain: while in the background stands the ruined fortress, as a reminder of the shift from castle to fortified manor house, from stern defence to greater luxury, which occurred everywhere in later medieval England and Wales.

See **Castles of the Norman Conquest.**

The ruinous fortifications at Tretower.

Tutbury is now a small and attractive market town by the river Dove, but once it was the headquarters of the barony of the powerful Norman lord, Henry de Ferrers. It was he who built the first castle, between 1066 and 1071, and founded the alien priory of St Mary in about 1080.

Only the motte and bailey earthworks remain of the first castle. The shell-keep which crowns the motte is not even medieval, but an eighteenth century folly. In the bailey are the remains of a free-standing twelfth century chapel, but most of the other masonry remains belong to the fifteenth century. It is therefore to the priory (now the parish church) that the visitor must go to find Norman architecture.

Although not as dominating as the castle, the church also occupies a fine elevated position and, like the town, it was once protected by the large earthwork enclosure (parts of which can still be seen) running to the south of the castle. Originally colonised by Benedic-tine monks from St Pierre-sur-Dives in Normandy, some of whom probably also served in the castle chapel, the existing church was founded in about 1100.

Much of the present building, however, dates from the late medieval or Victorian periods, and of the Norman church only the nave – originally a storey higher – and the south aisle survive. But the crowning glory of the Norman work is the west front, which ended the first building programme in about 1160. The west doorway is a masterpiece, flanked by imaginatively carved capitals with beasts and figures and surmounted by seven sculptured arches. The outermost arch is of particular interest, for it represents the earliest known use of alabaster in Britain. Mined in a quarry to the south-west of Tutbury, this easily carved material was to be much prized by later medieval sculptors for monuments and small religious panels or altarpieces: but here it makes a pioneering appearance.

TUTBURY Staffordshire
OS 128 SK 210293
Tutbury is four and a half miles north-west of Burton-on-Trent, on the A50: the castle is north-west of the town, by the river.

Canterbury

The city of Canterbury, one of the first places the Conqueror took on his march from Hastings to London in 1066, was a prize indeed: for it was (and still is) the undoubted ecclesiastical capital of England. Its pre-eminence dates from 597, when St Augustine came from Rome to convert the heathen Saxons, and founded here the very first Christian church and monastery in southern England. Shortly afterwards Augustine became its first archbishop, with power to appoint subordinate bishops as the work of conversion progressed: and ever since then the Archbishops of Canterbury have been the head of the English church.

At the time of the Conquest, however, the great office had an unworthy occupant – the wily, scandalous and much-excommunicated Stigand, appointed by William's old enemies the Godwinsons. As soon as he could, therefore, the Conqueror arranged Stigand's deposition, replacing him in 1070 by his own friend and leading ecclesiastical adviser Lanfranc of Bec. Though seventy years old, Lanfranc was a man of prodigious energy as well as piety: and at once he set about not only tripling the size of the monastery – which thus became the largest in England, with nearly 150 monks – but also completely rebuilding the Saxon cathedral, which had been badly damaged by fire in 1067.

Very little of Lanfranc's cathedral survives, but the surviving work of his successor Anselm includes one of the greatest glories both of Canterbury and of Anglo-Norman architecture, the great crypt. Begun in 1096 and completed by 1130, it is by far the largest Norman crypt in the country: and where most crypts are virtually underground, Canterbury's is built so high – thus necessitating the pronounced step between the western and eastern halves of the cathedral's interior – that it is filled with light from its own windows. It is full, too, of ornate pillars, whose capitals are wonderfully carved with fantastic beasts in combat and other subjects, held to be not only the best also the best-preserved collection of early Norman sculpture in Britain: and among its many other treasures are a complete set of still-glowing twelfth century wall paintings in the crypt side chapel of St Gabriel.

Anselm's crypt originally supported an early Norman choir, but of this only the shell and exterior features remain, including a notable Norman staircase-tower – topped by four tiers of arches and a pyramid roof – attached to the outside of the south-east transept. The present interior of the choir, however, was entirely constructed during the 1170s and 80s, as a result of two momentous events in Canterbury's history. The first occurred on the 29th of December 1170, when Archbishop Thomas Becket was murdered in the north transept of his own cathedral, at the place now called the Martyrdom. Once Henry II's closest associate and chancellor, Thomas had reluctantly accepted the archbishopric from him in 1162: but almost at once the two friends had fallen out, for Becket took his duties seriously and defended the Church against the king's encroachments. Finally, after a series of short-lived reconciliations, an hysterical outburst from Henry sent four household knights spurring to Canterbury, where they cut down the archbishop as he stood at his prayers. The king had to expiate this horrific sacrilege by submitting to a beating at Thomas's tomb, from which miracles were soon being reported: and in 1173 Becket was canonised, to become one of the most revered saints of medieval Britain.

A year later, in 1174, tragedy struck again when an accidental fire gutted the choir, facing the monks with the problem of how best to rebuild it as a fit setting for the martyr's shrine. The man they chose to do so, the master mason William of Sens, initiated a revolution in cathedral-building: for he introduced from his native France the new Early Gothic style of architecture, which in Canterbury Cathedral choir appears for the first time in England. Its hallmarks, there clearly to be seen, are taller and more slender pillars, a vaulted rather than a flat roof, a profusion of decorative columns of black Purbeck marble, and of course the pointed Gothic rather than the rounded Norman main arches. William's work, starting at the choir's west end, extends as far as the high altar, which he reached in 1179: but then a serious fall from the scaffolding forced his retirement, and he was succeeded by another William, called simply "the Englishman". The new architect continued eastwards, building the Trinity Chapel which was to house the shrine and rounding off the east end of the cathedral with the semi-circular Corona, or "Becket's Crown".

St Thomas's fabulous jewel-encrusted shrine, of course, was broken up at the Reformation – for Henry VIII did not love churchmen who resisted their king. Yet the beautiful twelfth century stained glass windows of the Trinity Chapel, where the shrine stood, still survive to proclaim the martyr's miracles. So too does the fine thirteenth century pavement which surrounded the tomb, while all about are the monuments of the great men – including Henry IV and the Black Prince – who sought to be buried as close as possible to what was regarded as the holiest place in England. To it flocked the Canterbury Pilgrims immortalised by Chaucer, and during the late fourteenth century their offerings helped the monks to rebuild Lanfranc's nave in the Perpendicular style, as we now see it: while in the early Tudor period they raised the lofty and majestic Bell Harry tower which dominates the whole city. For many visitors, nevertheless, Canterbury Cathedral's Norman crypt and choir still provide the most memorable experiences.

Much Norman work likewise survives in the vastly extensive monastic buildings of the cathedral priory, which lie immediately to the north of the cathedral itself. Lanfranc's dormitory, for example, stands on the eastern side of the fine fourteenth century vaulted cloister, which is accessible from the Martyrdom: while the infirmary buildings (accessible via door in the crypt) are also substantially Norman, notable among them being the unusual lavatory tower, which once housed a great cistern, part of the priory's elaborate waterworks. Norman also are the treasury near the north-east end of the cathedral, and the massive court gate at the north-west corner of the Green Court.

Elsewhere in the city, too, the Normans have left their mark. East of the cathedral precinct, and reached from it by passing through a memorial garden and a door in the towering city wall, and then crossing Broad Street, are the remains of St Augustine's Abbey. This, the cathedral priory's great rival, was the missionary saint's original seventh century monastery, the burial place of many early archbishops and Saxon kings of Kent. As so often happened, however, the Normans completely rebuilt it, and the remnants of the church begun by Abbot Scotland in 1070 are still to be seen.

Returning to the cathedral precinct, and now leaving it by its main or Christ Church Gate – ornately decorated with Tudor heraldry – the visitor should then walk straight ahead down narrow Mercery Lane into the High Street. Here turn right, and where the High Street becomes St Peter's Street (at a bridge over the Stour) is St Thomas's or Eastbridge Hospital, opening immediately onto the street. Built soon after the martyr's death, in 1180, this pilgrim hostel (now an almshouse) has a fine vaulted undercroft where the pilgrims slept, and above a chapel and a hall with an original wall-painting of Christ in Majesty.

Further out to the south-west (but also visible from the by-pass) is Canterbury Castle, a huge but sadly ruinous four-square Norman keep: it was probably built in the late eleventh century, perhaps to replace an earlier fortress which existed here before 1086.

A Benedictine priory was founded at Tynemouth in 1090 by Robert de Mowbray, Earl of Northumberland, on the site of a much earlier Saxon monastery. Initially he summoned monks from Durham, but after a quarrel dependence was transferred to St Albans Abbey. Once the largest and richest Benedictine house in Northumberland, Tynemouth was dissolved in 1539, although its fortified gatehouse and other defences encouraged Henry VIII to retain the site as a royal castle.

The setting is most dramatic – on a rocky promontory at the mouth of the river Tyne. Today, the two walls of the east end, still standing to their full height, look spectacular, stark against the skyline. In fact, although none of the earlier defences remain, the setting determined that the priory was as much fortress as monastery throughout the Middle Ages.

Excavations have revealed the plan of the priory (whose foundations are marked out in the grass) but of the earliest church only the tower pillars and fragments of the nave survive above ground. The chancel, whose walls still stand so high, was built in about 1200 and extended the east end of the church well beyond its original Norman limits: it was added to accommodate the increasing number of lucrative pilgrims to the priory's two shrines – those of St Oswin, a murdered Saxon king of Northumbria, and of St Henry of Coquet, a devout hermit and miracle-worker who died in 1127. Later still, in the mid-fifteenth century, the small but splendidly well-preserved Percy chantry, with its amazingly ornate ceiling and rose window, was also added to the east end by the Percy family, Dukes of Northumberland.

TYNEMOUTH PRIORY

Tyne and Wear
OS 88 NZ 374695
The priory is on the Northumberland coast, eight and a half miles east-north-east of Newcastle city centre by signposted roads, and three miles north-east of the north end of the Tyne Tunnel.

The fortified priory gatehouse, seen in the distance from the ruins of the church.

THE MOTE OF URR
Dumfries and Galloway
OS 84 NX 816648

The Mote is two and a half miles north of Dalbeattie, and visible across the Urr Water west of the B794 road from Dalbeattie to Haugh of Urr: it may be reached by turning east off the B794 at Netheryett, onto a track crossing the river to Milton of Buittle farm.

An Anglo-Norman adventurer, Walter de Berkeley, was granted lands here in the late twelfth century as a reward for his services in the reconquest of Galloway. Such men were not unusual in the Scottish court of David I, and their loyalty was retained by grants of land. The introduction of feudal management to many Scottish estates was an interesting consequence of this policy.

The motte and bailey castle was built on an artificial gravel mound between two natural channels of the Urr Water. A deep moat was added to strengthen the natural obstacles. Only the grassed-over motte now remains visible, but excavations have shown that the first castle consisted of a large timber keep or tower, defended by a palisade round the motte top. Stone turrets seem to have been added on the inner side of the palisade at an unknown date. Pottery from various excavations suggests that the castle remained in use until at least the fourteenth century.

WALTHAM ABBEY Essex
OS 166 TL 381007

The abbey is some fifteen miles north of central London, standing by the A121 in the centre of Waltham Abbey town. It is accessible from London via the A10 and the A121; or from the M25, turning off at junction 25 and going east on the A1010/A121. Two miles west of the abbey, at the junction of the A121 and A1010, is Waltham Cross, one of the "Eleanor Crosses" commemorating Edward I's queen.

The town of Waltham Abbey lies to the north-east of Enfield and close to the M25. The former abbey church is now the parish of Holy Cross and St Laurence, and is situated at the west end of the town.

Looking at the outside of the abbey, it requires a certain amount of imagination to appreciate the scale of Earl (later King) Harold's great church, founded in the years immediately before the Norman Conquest. However, once inside, the great columns and arch at the east end immediately indicate that this was once a church of considerable importance. The existing structure formed the nave of the Norman church, but little of the fabric dates with certainty from Harold's time, perhaps only an area of stonework in herringbone pattern (in the west wall of the south transept). It has been suggested, however, that Waltham could be a pre-Conquest church built in Norman style; since Harold would have become familiar with Norman architecture when, before he became king, he visited Duke William in France. But it is possible, conversely, that only the east part of the church was complete in 1066, the nave and aisles not being finished until the twelfth century. The arch which now frames the east window was one of four supporting a great central tower. There has been some restoration of the magnificent decorated columns and arches: and the twelfth century south doorway, with elaborately carved capitals inside, has been substantially reconstructed.

Harold plainly took a great personal interest in the foundation. As king he prayed here on his way south to Hastings and reputedly received an ill omen for the coming conflict, when the figure of Christ on the cross lowered its head. After the defeat, Harold's mutilated body was brought back here and buried, traditionally by the high altar. A modern stone is set in the grass of the churchyard on the site of the altar as his memorial (to the east of the standing church).

The church was refounded in the late twelfth century by Henry II as an Augustinian priory, and within a few years it was promoted to become the abbey from which the town derived its name. The destruction of the east end was not the work of vindictive Normans – the edifice stood for centuries, eventually falling victim to Henry VIII's policy of Dissolution in the 1530s. The nave was then saved because the local people claimed it as their parish church.

The Domesday Book

The Domesday survey was compiled just twenty years after the Norman Conquest and one year before William the Conqueror's death. It is a unique document, for no similar survey has ever been attempted. Within its folios some 13,000 places are named, many of them for the first time. It is therefore not surprising that for many towns, villages and hamlets, 1086 represents the starting point of their history.

Domesday is the earliest public record, and was preserved by the officers of the king's household for more than eight centuries. By 1176 it was already known by its popular name Domesday, because of the finality of its testimony in all disputes with the Crown. By then it was in daily use at the Royal Exchequer. It remained unpublished, however, until the very end of the eighteenth century, since when it has become the focus of attention of much research by the foremost scholars in Norman history.

According to the famous "Anglo-Saxon Chronicle", the Domesday survey first arose from detailed discussions which William had with his councillors in Gloucester at Christmas 1085:

"The King spent Christmas with his councillors at Gloucester and held court there for five days, which was followed by a three-day synod by the archbishop and the clergy . . . After this the King had important deliberations and exhaustive discussions with his council about this land and how it was peopled and with what sort of men. Then he sent his men all over England into every shire to ascertain how many hundreds of "hides" of land there were in each shire, and how much land and livestock the King himself owned in the country, and what annual dues were lawfully his from each shire. He also had recorded how much land his archbishops had, and his diocesan bishops, his abbots and his earls, had . . . and what or how much each man who was a land holder here in England had in land, or in livestock, and how much money it was worth. So very thoroughly did he have the inquiry carried out that there was not a single "hide", not one virgate of land, not even – it is shameful to record it but it did not seem shameful for him to do – not even one ox, not one cow, nor one pig which escaped notice in the survey. And all the surveys were subsequently brought to him."

[*Anglo-Saxon Chronicle:* trans. G. N. Garmonsway]

The survey was carried out in 1086 and the final record probably completed by the time of William's death in September 1087. Although we know what was actually done and how it was done, the reasons why this massive inquiry was set in train are not really clear. One of the possible motives behind the survey may have been the confusion and alarm caused by a threatened Scandinavian invasion of England. William was obliged to recruit a large force of mercenary troops from Northern France, which he billeted on the lands of his barons in 1085. This action may have caused the king to realise that he did not know the full resources of his kingdom, or the exact economic and territorial position of his powerful barons. Furthermore, although England had been shared out between the royal favourites, many estates had been unlawfully acquired and were illegally held in 1086. The compilation of Domesday Book under sworn evidence seems to have been a means of rectifying that particular problem. It has also been suggested that the Domesday Book was a *geld* or taxation book, drawn up in order to substantially increase royal revenues. The artificial nature of many of the Domesday entries suggests that this may well have been one of the reasons behind it.

The Book is in fact two volumes, the *Great Domesday* (Volume One) and the *Little Domesday* (Volume Two). Both are now preserved in the Public Record Office in Chancery Lane, London. Volume One, written at Winchester in 1086, is the survey of thirty English counties, whilst Volume Two is only half the size and contains the entries for just three East Anglian counties – Norfolk, Suffolk and Essex. However, it is more detailed than the first volume and compiled by a number of different scribes. There is also a third document, the *Exon Domesday*, which is an early draft of the Survey made by the king's commissioners for the south-western counties of Devon, Cornwall, Somerset, Wiltshire and Dorset. This is again more detailed than Volume One, and is preserved in Exeter Cathedral where it was no doubt written.

The good fortune which has left us with three original documents of the survey has also provided us with a contemporary account of its under-taking, also written in 1086, by Robert, Bishop of Hereford:

"the twentieth year of his reign, by order of William, King of the English, there was made a survey of the whole of England, that is to say, of the lands of the several provinces of England, and of the possessions of each and all of the magnates. This was done in respect of plough land and habitations and of men both bond and free, both those who dwelt in cottages and those who had houses and some arable land; and in respect of ploughs and horses and other animals; and in respect of the services and payments due from all men in the whole land. Other investigators followed the first; and men were sent into provinces which they did not know, and where they were them-selves unknown, in order that they might be given the opportunity of checking the first survey, and, if necessary, of denouncing its authors as guilty to the king. And the land was vexed with many calamities arising from the collection of the royal money."

[trans. W. H. Stevenson]

The survey was undertaken by the king's commissioners or "investi-gators" who were responsible to him alone. Again we are lucky to have another document, known as the "*Ely Inquiry*", which provides a vital clue as to how the survey was carried out and what information the king wanted recorded.

"Here follows the inquest of lands, as the King's barons made it, to wit: by the oath of the sheriff of the shire and of all the barons and their Frenchmen and of the whole Hundred, of the priest, the reeve, and six villagers of each village. In order; What is the manor called? Who held it in the time of King Edward (the Confessor)? Who now holds it? How many hides? How many ploughs on the demesne? How many men? How many villagers? How many cottars? How many slaves? How many freemen? How many socmen? How much wood? How much meadow? How much pasture? How many mills? How many fishponds? How much has been added or taken away? How much, taken together, it was worth and how much now? How much each freeman or socman had or has? All this at three dates, to wit in the time of King Edward, and when King William gave it, and as it is now. And if it is possible for more to be had than is had."

This information is presented in each of the three volumes, shire by shire, and within each shire is given the holdings of the king and then of his tenants-in-chief. Also at this time each shire was divided into administrative units called hundreds – which consisted of a number of manors. It is more than likely that the king's commissioners received the results of their enquiries from the chosen representatives of each hundred, who were sworn under oath when giving their testimonies at the shire courts. All the returns from certainly the counties surveyed for Volume One were then brought to the *scriptorium* at Winchester, where the monks sorted the mass of information into some sort of order. A typical entry in the survey is one for Sherborne St John, in Hampshire:

"Hugh de Port holds SHERBORNE (St John) from the King. Wulfeva held it from King Edward; she could go whither she would. Then it answered for ten hides; now for seven hides. Land for ten ploughs. In lordship three ploughs; sixteen villagers and nineteen smallholders with five ploughs. A church with half a hide pays 20s; five slaves; three mills at 27s 6d; meadow, twenty acres. Value before 1066 and later £10; now £15".

However, from other contemporary and later evidence, it is plain that even within their terms of reference the king's commissioners did not always give a full account. There are a number of gaps within the areas covered; some districts were left out entirely, particularly in the north and south-west; and among the many towns omitted were the capitals, London and Winchester. There are also tantalising glimpses of urban life in places not thought to be towns in the eleventh century, from references to markets and tolls in some entries. Nevertheless, even with all its imperfections, the Domesday Book remains a unique and astonishing record, which has enabled us to deduce a very great deal about the life and conditions in Norman England, both before and at the time of its compilation.

WARKWORTH CASTLE
Northumberland
OS 81 NU 247058

The beautiful village of Warkworth is twenty-six miles north of Newcastle and seven miles south-east of Alnwick (which also has a fine medieval castle). It is reached from Alnwick via the A1068, and from Newcastle via the A1, the B6345 eastwards through Felton, and the A1068 north through Amble. Half a mile west of the village is Warkworth Hermitage, a house and chapel cut out of solid rock for a fourteenth century hermit.

Right, the passage of time serves to reveal the structural detail of the Norman gatehouse. Below, the entrance to the castle, with the upper storey of the palatial fifteenth-century keep beyond, to the right.

A motte and bailey castle is known to have existed here by 1158, when Henry II granted the castle and the manor to Roger Fitz Richard, whose family held it for the next 200 years. It was probably built by Henry, son of King David I of Scotland, who had been created Earl of Northumberland in 1139, but it is possible that he merely strengthened an earlier fortification.

The castle is strategically placed on high ground rising above a loop in the River Coquet, and the main village street climbs steeply southward from the fortified bridge (with its rare survival of a towered gate) to the gates of the castle. The only level approach to the castle is on the south side, which is guarded by a deep moat, curtain wall, flanking towers, gatehouse and drawbridge. Today the setting of the castle and the pretty unspoilt village is quite delightful, but the peaceful atmosphere belies the more turbulent past hinted at by the towering ruins.

The castle was in use from the twelfth until the sixteenth century, and has some interesting medieval masonry: but there was so much rebuilding that little remains of the Norman fortress, apart from its motte and bailey plan, part of the east curtain wall and the west wall foundations of the hall. The magnificent early fifteenth century keep, however, is definitely worth exploring.

There is also a large and fairly complete Norman church here, which has windows

dating from about 1100 on the nave north side: while in the chancel there is some fine chevron work on the rib vaulting.

The fine Norman church stands apart from, and to the north of, the present village. On the south and east sides of the churchyard are pronounced earthworks associated with the Norman manor house. In 1108, the manor was sold by Archbishop Thomas of York to Herbert, chamberlain to King Henry I and father of Saint William of York. Herbert built the present church between about 1110 and 1120, and this pious labour is commemorated by the Latin inscription on the sundial above the south door. This translates "in honour of the Apostle St Andrew, Herbert of Winchester built this in the time of (...)".. His son, when Archbishop of York (1143–54), gave the church to the Prior of Nostell, who in 1268 gave it to the Dean and Chapter of York. The building was restored in 1872.

Other Norman features of note are the tall west tower on the outside: and, internally, both the tower and the chancel arches; the round-headed doors and windows; and the fine patterned drum-shaped font.

Left, this sundial over Weaverthorpe church's south door records the founder's name, and just within is the Norman drum-shaped font.

WEAVERTHORPE
North Yorkshire
OS 101 SE 966711

Weaverthorpe lies amid the bare rolling hills of the Yorkshire Wolds, some twenty-five miles north-east of York and nine miles north of Driffield. From York it may be reached by turning south off the A64 York-Scarborough road at Sherburn, or more scenically via the A166 Bridlington road, the B1251 through Sledmere, and a minor road turning north.

WEST MALLING Kent
OS 188 TQ 683576

West Malling (locally "mawling") is five miles west of Maidstone, via the A25 and the A228: it can also be reached from the M20 motorway, leaving at junction 4 and travelling south on the A228. St Leonard's Tower (TQ 675570) is half a mile south of the church, by the A228.

This small but charming Kentish town contains a wealth of attractive buildings, spanning a period from shortly after the Conquest to the eighteenth century. At one end of the town lies the parish church of St Mary, where a late Victorian restoration of the nave has been pleasingly blended with the Norman chancel and tower, while at the other is Malling Abbey, founded by Bishop Gundulf in about 1090. Parts of its monastic buildings (closed to the public) are now once again occupied by nuns.

The main Norman work surviving at the abbey is the west tower, which originally may have formed part of a grander west facade. The arcaded angle turrets clearly date from the late eleventh century, the bottom two tiers being built of tufa whilst the upper part is of Caen stone, a dignified and beautiful stone imported from Normandy. Note that the shafts of the arcading below the pinnacles have "waterleaf" capitals, and thus should be dated to the very end of the twelfth century. The occasion for this rebuilding was a great fire in 1190 which destroyed much of the tower and the abbey. Rebuilding began at once, and the new abbey church was modelled on the style of Rochester cathedral.

The abbey tower may be compared with the well-preserved Norman keep tower, St Leonard's, which stands half a mile southwest of the town. Its plain windows are set amid blank arches, and its stair turret is incorporated in an enlarged north-west buttress. The function of St Leonard's tower has been a matter of some controversy: but it appears to have been built by Bishop Gundulf at Rochester in about 1100, to control the local road systems.
See Rochester.

WHITE CASTLE Gwent
OS 161 SO 380168

The castle is five and a half miles north-east of Abergavenny, via the B4233 road to Monmouth and a signposted road turning northward at Llantilio Crossenny. This is an area full of castles: within a radius of six miles from White Castle are Grosmont (on the B4347 to the north); Skenfrith (on the B4521, to the east) and magnificent Raglan (to the south, on the A40).

Splendidly set against a mountain backcloth, with its towers rising above deep water-filled moats, White Castle is among the most romantic of British castles: and it must have appeared even more like a fairy-tale fortress when it was coated with the gleaming white plaster which gave it its name, and which still survives in sheltered crannies among the walls.

Exactly when the first stronghold was built here is uncertain, but one undoubtedly existed by the mid twelfth century. This had probably already assumed its present plan of an oval inner ward encircled by a moat, flanked and protected on one side by a crescent-shaped "hornwork" (likewise moated) and on the other by an outer bailey, also with a moat of its own. Each of these three artificial islands was originally defended by wooden stockades, while the inner ward also possessed a small rectangular stone tower, whose foundations still survive. Next, probably in about 1185, the stockade round the inner ward was replaced by a formidable but at first untowered stone wall, which still exists virtually complete.

Then, probably during a period of acute tension between English and Welsh in 1267–77, the entire castle was immensely strengthened. This was done by adding four massive protruding circular towers to the plain inner bailey wall, so designed that their crossfire could sweep every inch of intervening "dead ground": and by constructing a formidable new twin-towered gatehouse to cover the inner ward's entrance. And at the same time, an entirely new stone curtain wall – also equipped with its own circular towers and great gatehouse – was built to defend the outer bailey, the "island" to the north-east of the inner ward.

Such round towers and mighty gatehouse keeps, a decade or so later, were to become a familiar feature of King Edward I's great castles – Rhuddlan, Conway, Harlech and the rest – in north Wales: so it comes as no great surprise that the refortification of White Castle was all but certainly the work of Edward himself, then heir to the throne and defending his father's frontiers against the Welsh.

See **Castles of the Norman Conquest.**

The inner gatehouse and round-towered walls of White Castle rise above deep water-filled moats.

Apart perhaps from London, Winchester was the most important town in England at the time of the Norman Conquest. The historic capital of Wessex, it remained the centre of royal administration and the home of the vital treasury: and as such it became the focus of a considerable building programme in the later eleventh and early twelfth centuries. As usual, much of this construction work – a castle, a bishop's palace, and a huge new cathedral – was symbolic as well as practical.

The cathedral, indeed, is of immense length – at 556 feet, it is the longest in England and in fact (save for St Peter's in Rome) the longest in Europe – and this was intended from the first. It was begun in 1079 by the Norman bishop Walkelin, to replace the earlier "Old Minster", one of three great Saxon churches crowded together on this site: and of Walkelin's building the underground crypt, the transepts, and part of the monastic cloister still survive. The transepts are massive and powerfully built, yet neither so massive nor so expertly constructed as the neighbouring pillars of the central tower, beneath which lies the tomb of the Conqueror's son King William Rufus, buried here after his mysterious death in the New Forest in 1100. For, seven years after this event – and, according to legend, as a belated protest against the burial of the wicked monarch beneath it – Bishop Walkelin's original tower collapsed: and when a replacement was built, the huge supporting pillars were designed to prevent this from following its predecessor's example.

The remainder of this great cathedral – which also enshrines the bones of many Anglo-Saxon kings, in tomb-chests raised above the choir – was remodelled in later medieval times, though the Norman font of black Tournai marble survives in the nave. So too, outside the church to the south (and almost the sole survivor of the cathedral priory's monastic buildings) does the early Norman entrance of the chapter house, a large round arch flanked by four smaller ones, all supported by pillars with scalloped capitals.

Wolvesey Palace, two hundred yards south-east of the cathedral, was built by Bishop Henry of Blois in 1130–40: the parts of the building which date from that period (including the original gatehouse) being on the north side of the site. Described by contemporaries as "a house like a palace with a very strong tower", Wolvesey possessed its own square keep, whose remains stand at the south end of the great hall: some 140 feet long, this hall was built in the 1170s, and apparently resembled the hall at the Bishop of Winchester's other palace at Bishop's Waltham. Such buildings reflect the wealth of Winchester's prelates, in medieval times much the richest bishops in England.

Winchester also had a royal castle, on the site to the west of the city now occupied by the county offices: but little Norman work now survives there save the earthworks and the excavated remains of the eleventh century keep, near Henry III's thirteenth century great hall with its "King Arthur's Round Table".

South of the city, just off the A33, stands the Hospital of St Cross (SU 476278), pleasantly reached on foot by a walk of about a mile along the Water Meadows. This was founded in 1136 by the palace-building Bishop Henry of Blois, but the present hospital church – large, high-roofed and cross-shaped – apparently dates from the turn of the twelfth and thirteenth centuries, and represents an excellent example of the transition from the late Norman to the Early English style of architecture. The hospital, moreover, still fulfils its intended role as an almshouse – one of the oldest of such institutions in Britain: and continues, uniquely, to distribute a daily "wayfarer's dole" of bread and beer to all comers. But travellers wishing to sample Bishop Henry's largesse should apply early in the day, for the allotted supply soon runs out.

WINCHESTER Hampshire
OS 185 SU 482292
Winchester is sixty-six miles south-west of London, via the M3 and A33. The cathedral and Wolvesey Palace are in the city centre, the castle remains to the west, and St Cross Hospital outside the city to the south, near the A33 by-pass. Visitors should also see famous Winchester School (near the cathedral) begun by Bishop William of Wykeham in 1387: parts of the largely medieval buildings are generally open to the public.

Opposite, Bishop Henry of Blois' Norman marble font in Winchester Cathedral.

Very little of the magnificent structure which forms the present day Windsor Castle is Norman, and even the "Norman Gateway" is an impostor, being fourteenth century in date! Norman work, however, is clearly visible in the layout of the defences.

The castle was erected in about 1070 by William the Conqueror to defend the strategic reaches of the middle Thames Valley, and consisted of an unusual motte and bailey, with narrow enclosed areas to make use of the lengthy chalk escarpment. All the ditches were dry, and the castle was divided by a central motte (the Middle Ward) into Upper and Lower Wards.

The present castle still follows the outline-plan of these two wards, although no Norman domestic buildings survive within them: and the huge central motte (250 feet in diameter at its base) also remains to be seen, albeit much landscaped. This motte was originally crowned with wooden structures, but in 1165–71 Henry II replaced these in stone, and part of his work is still visible in the present great Round Tower – in fact oval in plan – which yet dominates the castle. The stonework as far as the coping above the large windows dates from the 1170s, the rest being nineteenth century. The curtain wall between the north terrace and the Round Tower is also twelfth century.

Much of the existing stonework of the walls around the Upper Ward likewise dates from this period of building, although the walls and towers of the Lower Ward were left unfinished when Henry's rebellious sons were defeated, and were only completed some sixty years later.

WINDSOR CASTLE Berkshire
OS 175 SU 970770
Windsor is twenty miles west of London via the M4, leaving at junction 6. The huge castle, a favourite residence of Britain's monarchs, dominates the town and surrounding area: among its attractions are St George's Chapel, burial place of kings and home of the Order of the Garter; and the royal apartments (closed when the Queen is in residence). Nearby is Eton College, with another famous chapel.

Few of the other buildings in this enormous castle have Norman work, there having been substantial alterations in the fourteenth and the fifteenth century (when St George's Chapel was built) and a massive restoration undertaken in 1820–30 by King George IV, who is responsible for much of the present appearance of the castle.

Windsor Great Park represents the remains of an extensive royal forest which existed to the south and west of the castle, and was used for hunting by Saxon, Norman and medieval kings.

WORCESTER CATHEDRAL
Worcestershire
OS 150 SO 849545

Worcester is 120 miles north-west of London, via the M40 and the A44. The cathedral stands near the centre of the city, by the Severn and off Deansway, and contains the splendid tomb of the much-maligned King John.

A cathedral was established at Worcester in about 680, and was originally served by a mixed community of monks and secular clergy. This community was virtually defunct by the early tenth century: but in about 969, as part of the revival of the English church, it was re-founded as a Benedictine abbey by its bishop Oswald, later canonised. Thus it remained, although also the seat of the bishop, until the Dissolution of the Monasteries, when it was reconstituted as a cathedral served by a dean and chapter.

increased from twelve to fifty. Like his Norman contemporaries, Wulfstan felt the need to rebuild on a massive scale, and under his direction all traces of the pre-Conquest church (already badly damaged by the Danes in 1041) were swept away, the only possible survival being the re-used shafts in the arcading of the slype (next to the chapter house).

The most impressive part of Wulfstan's cathedral still extant is the crypt, built to house the relics of St Oswald. It has a semi-circular apse, and its serried ranks of pillars with their

The earliest part of the present building dates from the episcopate of St Wulfstan (1062–1095), one of the leading figures of the late Anglo-Saxon church and the only Anglo-Saxon bishop not replaced by a Norman after the Conquest. Under him the church at Worcester flourished, and the number of monks at the cathedral priory

cushion capitals, supporting the groin vaulting, make this one of the finest Norman crypts in Britain. What is also interesting is that the plan of the crypt almost certainly mirrors the design of the late eleventh century chancel above, destroyed when the present magnificent choir was aded in the mid thirteenth century. The only other survivals from Wulfstan's church are the two round-headed arches in the east walls of the transepts, which led into apsidal chapels flanking the chancel. Also not to be missed are the two western bays of the nave. These date from around 1170, and although the chevron ornament and the decoration on the capitals is purely Norman in inspiration, the use of the pointed arch is one of the earliest examples of Gothic architecture in England.

Norman work in the cloister includes the early twelfth century chapter house, with its unusually slender central pillar and blank arcading on its walls; and the undercroft beneath the refectory in the south range. An unusual feature of the cloisters is that the difficulties of water supply, and the siting of a castle on what is now Castle Green, meant that the monk's dormitory and its reredorter (latrines) had to be laid out at right-angles to the west range, towards the River Severn, rather than in the east range as is customary. The ruins of the infirmary can also still be seen, to the south-west of the west front of the cathedral.

Far left, this slender central pillar supports the roof of Worcester Cathedral's late Norman chapter house which was used as a library by the Victorians and is used by the Cathedral and town choirs as their practice room today. Left, Bishop Wulfstan's beautiful crypt, beneath the choir.

Worksop is fifteen miles east of Sheffield. It can easily be reached from the A1 (four miles away) by turning west on the A619, or from the M1 by turning east on the same road at junction 30.

The yew-wood south door of Worksop Priory has fine iron scroll-work, and within is an impressive late Norman nave, far right.

Worksop lay close to the northern boundary of Sherwood Forest, one of the great royal hunting grounds established by the Norman kings and based on the royal manor of Mansfield. Sherwood has been famous since the mid fourteenth century as the home of Robin Hood, and the priory church contains a skull with an arrowhead embedded in it – a gruesome link with medieval legend.

Worksop Priory (formerly Radford Priory) was founded in 1103 by William de Lovetot as a priory for Augustinian canons, and the priory church of Our Lady and St Cuthbert is still used for parish worship. The plain west front with its recessed door belongs to the early twelfth century, and its shallow buttresses follow the fashion of eleventh century Normandy. It is earlier in date than the other Norman part of the church, the nave, which belongs to the late twelfth century and has vaulted aisles and rounded nave churches, all rather tediously covered with repetitive nail-head carving. As in many other major Anglo-Norman churches of this date, the nave contains a gallery and clerestory. The south door, which may be of late Norman date, is made of yew from Sherwood Forest and is covered with rich iron scroll-work.

The church is the high spot of the priory remains, and few other monastic buildings survive: these mainly date from the 1140s, with the exception of the fine fourteenth century gate-house with its unique wayside shrine and chapel.

In 1068–69, after a series of revolts, William I built two castles to the south-east of the city, one on each bank of the River Ouse. These are represented today by two flat-topped earthen mounds or mottes, one beneath Clifford's Tower (SE 606515) and the other at the Old Baile (SE 603513), approximately facing each other across Victorian Skeldergate Bridge. While it is not known which of the two mounds is the earlier or, indeed, how they related to the earthen rampart that protected the city, they are significant in their own right. For the earliest documented castles of the Norman Conquest recorded with fully-developed mottes are those built during William's northern campaigns of 1068–69, and the York castles fall into this group.

On the west bank of the Ouse, overlooking the junction of Skeldergate and Bishopgate Street, stands the motte of Baile Hill, known as "The Old Baile" since at least 1268. Excavations here in 1968 revealed steps cut into the side of the motte leading up to a timber building on top, surrounded by a palisade. The site has been much disturbed by four-teenth century wall-building, and the con-struction of a Civil War gun-emplacement, and today it is tree-covered.

The motte of Clifford's Tower, on the east

YORK North Yorkshire
OS 105 SE 606515
York is 193 miles north of London, via the A1 and A64. The two mottes are near the centre of the city, Clifford's Tower being adjacent to the Castle Museum, famous for the Victorian streets rebuilt within. A major tourist centre, York's many attractions also include the great Minster; the walls; the Jorvik Viking Museum; the National Railway Museum; the Yorkshire Museum with the nearby ruins of thirteenth-century St Mary's Abbey; and eighteen medieval parish churches.

123

bank and now flanked by the buildings of the Castle Museum, was also originally defended by a palisade and crowned by a wooden keep. In the mid thirteenth century, however, this was replaced by Clifford's Tower itself, a stone quatrefoil (or four-lobed) keep whose shape is unique in Britain.

The Norman city defences of York consisted not of a stone-built wall, but almost entirely of a high earthen rampart raised over successive Roman, Anglian and Anglo-Danish defensive circuits: a situation best appreciated near the "Anglian Tower" behind the public library buildings, where a section of the bank has beeen cut away to reveal the succession of fortifications lying one above the other. The Norman earthwork ramparts, however, were pierced by stone gateways, some of which remained in use when the famous medieval stone walls which now surround York were constructed: Norman arches, for example, are incorporated into three of the present city gates (or "bars"), namely Bootham, Micklegate and Walmgate Bars.

Elsewhere in York – apart from the (signposted) remains of a late Norman house off Stonegate – there is comparatively little to see above ground of the Norman period. But beneath the great Gothic Minster lie the foundations of an earlier Norman cathedral, begun in 1070 and altered in the later twelfth century: and beneath the present Minster choir are the accessible and fascinating remains of a once-magnificent Norman crypt.

The Norman crypt beneath York Minster choir is well worth seeking out.

The tree-covered 'Old Baile', one of the Conqueror's mottes, seen from York's medieval walls.

GLOSSARY

Carved capital at Iffley.

An arcade at Much Wenlock.

The fine fount at East Meon.

ABBEY An independent monastery ruled by its own abbot or abbess, as opposed to a dependent *priory*.

AISLES Where a *chancel*, *nave* or *transept* is divided up by rows of pillars, the aisles are the corridor-like sections flanking the central space.

ALIEN PRIORY A *priory* dependent on and belonging to an *abbey* outside Britain.

AMBULATORY Semi-circular *aisle* leading round an *apse*.

APSE The semi-circular end of a church, or of a chapel in a church.

ARCADE A row of arches, generally supported on pillars: see *blank arcading*.

ASHLAR Fine masonry composed of large and carefully-shaped rectangular blocks.

BAILEY Walled enclosure of a castle, generally containing various buildings.

BAY Internal division of a building, separated from others by pillars etc. rather than solid walls.

BLANK ARCADING Decorative rows of arches carved in relief on a wall.

CANONS, REGULAR Groups of priests following a monastic rule and living together in an *abbey* or *priory*: in practice almost indistinguishable from *monks*.

CANONS, SECULAR Priests serving a cathedral or other great church, but owning property and neither bound by a monastic rule nor necessarily living communally.

CAPITALS The block-like heads of columns or pillars, often shaped or sculptured.

CHANCEL The part of the east end of a church where the main altar is placed, or sometimes the whole eastern half of the church. See also *choir*.

CHAPTER HOUSE The building in a monastery or cathedral where the monks or cathedral clergy met to discuss business, and in the case of monks to hear a chapter of the monastic rule.

CHOIR Strictly, the part of a church where services are said or sung. Sometimes used as a synonym for *chancel*.

CLERESTORY Uppermost storey of a church wall, generally containing windows and thus a "clear-storey".

CLOISTER In practice, used to mean the courtyard of a monastery, often surrounded by a covered walk where the monks took exercise.

COLLEGIATE CHURCH A large church, of less than cathedral status, served by a number of secular *canons*.

CORBELS Blocks of stone projecting from a wall, supporting the eaves of a roof or some other feature. Often decorated with carving.

CROSSING Space near the centre of a church, where the *chancel*, *nave* and *transepts* meet. In larger churches, the space under the central tower.

CRYPT Underground chamber beneath a church, generally at its east end.

CURTAIN WALL Stretch of plain wall between the towers of a castle or other fortification.

DECORATED Style of Gothic architecture which flourished in England from *c*.1280 until *c*.1340.

EARLY ENGLISH Style of architecture (also called early

OF TERMS

Gothic) which flourished in England during the thirteenth century, from the end of the Norman period until *c.*1280.

FOREBUILDING Block of building attached to a castle keep, covering its entrance like a porch and thus providing additional security.

GALLERY Upper storey of a church's interior wall, generally composed of rows of arches, between the main *arcade* and the *clerestory*. Also called a triforium.

GARDEROBE Individual privy or lavatory, often a small cell built into the thickness of a wall.

INFIRMARY Monastic building accommodating sick or aged monks.

KEEP Building which constituted the principal and innermost strongpoint of a castle, often a massive tower.

LANCET Slender window topped by a pointed arch.

LAY BROTHERS Inferior grade of *monks*, generally uneducated and occupied mainly with manual work.

MOAT Ditch protecting a castle or other fortification, sometimes but not always filled with water.

MONKS Men (not necessarily priests) living an enclosed life of poverty, chastity and obedience in a monastic *abbey* or *priory*.

MOTTE Artificial earthen mound forming the strongpoint of an early Norman castle. At first defended by wooden palisades and bearing timber structures, many were subsequently refortified in stone.

NAVE Western section of a church, generally used to provide space for the congregation.

PERPENDICULAR Latest style of Gothic architecture, flourishing in England from *c.*1335 to *c.*1530.

PIER Solid support for a major arch, sometimes square in section but often a pillar.

PRECINCT Enclosed or semi-enclosed space containing monastic buildings, or surrounding a cathedral.

PRESBYTERY In larger churches, the section lying east of the choir and containing the high altar. So called because it was reserved for priests.

PRIORY A dependent monastery ruled by a prior or prioress, but technically subordinate to the abbot of a greater house. Cathedral priories were so called because their nominal abbot was the bishop or archbishop.

REFECTORY Room where monks ate communally.

RERE-DORTER Monastic building containing latrines.

RETROCHOIR In a large church, the section "behind the choir" i.e. east of the high altar.

SEDILIA Seating by the altar, often of carved stone and built into a wall, for priests officiating at services.

SOLAR Private living room occupied by the owner of a castle or medieval house.

TRANSEPT The transverse projections, or "arms", of a cross-shaped church. Some very large churches have two sets of transepts, forming a "cross of Lorraine" plan.

TYMPANUM (plural TYMPANA) In Norman doorways, the semi-circular space between the horizontal lintel of the door and the arch above it. Often elaborately carved.

UNDERCROFT Vaulted basement, often semi-subterranean.

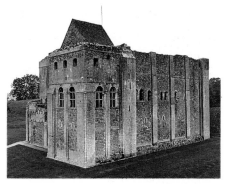

Keep and forebuilding at Castle Rising.

Nave of Kirkstall Abbey.

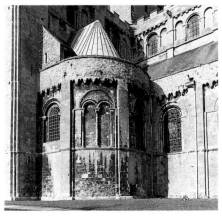

Apsed chapel at Romsey.

FURTHER READING

Brown, R. Allen, *The Normans and the Norman Conquest*, Constable, 1969
Douglas, D. C., *William the Conqueror*, Eyre Methuen, 1964
Douglas, D. C., *The Norman Achievement*, Eyre and Spottiswoode, 1969
Poole, A. L., *From Domesday Book to Magna Carta*, Oxford, 1964
Renn, D., *Norman Castles in Britain*, John Baker, 1973
Rowley, R. T., *The Norman Heritage*, Routledge, 1983
Stenton, Sir Frank, *Anglo-Saxon England*, Oxford, 1971

Spectator Publications wish gratefully to acknowledge the assistance provided to them by the clergy, the staff, and all the voluntary helpers in the many churches visited in the course of preparing this book. In particular, thanks go to the Vicar of Worksop for his kindness, and to the organist at the church of St John the Baptist, Adel, without whose timely appearance the interior photography done there would not have been possible. Permission to reproduce the photograph of Oakham Castle was kindly granted by the Leicestershire Museums, Art Galleries and Records Service.